The Journey of Prophet Muhammad

*Discovering Islam Through the Quran |
Duas and Insights for a Meaningful
Muslim Life – Islamic Books*

Hamza Al-Siddiq

ISBN : 9798879586527

Table of Contents

Chapter 4: Health and Harmony: Duas for Physical and Spiritual Well-being 38

Chapter 5: Self-Improvement Journey: Duas for Personal Development 48

Chapter 6: Community Well-being: Duas for Social Responsibility and Engagement 57

BONUS

Dear Reader,

We thank you for supporting us in carrying the message of Allah to the world.

We regularly have further updates on other projects and would be happy if you subscribe to our newsletter:

A positive surprise and our thanks are waiting for you.

Introduction

In the journey of faith, the words we whisper to our Creator in the quiet moments of our days and nights hold immense power. This book is a testament to the timeless act of turning to Allah in supplication, seeking His guidance, mercy, and blessings through the words of the Prophet Muhammad (peace be upon him) and the divine wisdom of the Quran.

This book is not merely a collection of invocations; it is a compass for the contemporary believer navigating the complexities of modern life while striving to remain anchored in their faith. Each chapter unfolds a tapestry of themes central to the human experience—morning rituals, protection, faith, health, self-improvement, community welfare, daily challenges, reflective times, religious obligations, praise, interpersonal relationships, success, and, uniquely, words of inspiration for exceptional circumstances.

The duas, presented in their original Arabic script, with Latin transcription and English translation, serve as a bridge connecting the heart of the believer to the compassion and mercy of Allah. These invocations are more than just phrases to be uttered; they are conversations with Allah, expressing our deepest desires, fears, hopes, and gratitude. From the invocations for a blessed start in the morning to the prayers for guidance and light, each dua has been carefully selected to enrich the spiritual practice of individuals seeking solace and strength in their Creator. The inclusion of inspirational Quranic interpretations offers insights that illuminate the path of understanding and reflection.

As you embark on this journey through the pages of this book, may you find in each chapter a reflection of your own quest for peace, a guide for your spiritual journey, and a reminder of the boundless grace and mercy that Allah extends to those who turn to Him. This book is an invitation to deepen your connection with Allah, to embrace the wisdom of the Prophet Muhammad (peace be upon him), and to live a life enriched by the transformative power of dua. May your hearts find peace, your minds gain clarity, and your souls achieve tranquility through the blessings of these prayers. And may you always be reminded that, in every moment of need or gratitude, turning to Allah with a sincere heart is the most profound action of faith. Welcome to a journey of faith, reflection, and spiritual growth.

Chapter 1:
Morning Duas: Invocations
for a Blessed Start

Dua for Waking Up

الحَمْدُ لِلَّهِ الَّذِي أَحْيَانَا بَعْدَ مَا أَمَاتَنَا وَإِلَيْهِ النُّشُورُ

Alhamdu lillahil-ladhi ahyana ba'da ma amatana wa-ilayhin-nushoor

Praise be to Allah who gave us life after He made us die, and to Him is the eventual coming.

Source: Sahih al-Bukhari 6311

Story of Wisdom:

إِنَّ أَبْرَهَةَ الحَبَشِيَّ أَرَادَ أَنْ يَهْدِمَ الكَعْبَةَ فَأَعَدَّ لِذَلِكَ الفِيلَ وَجَمَعَ النَّاسَ ثُمَّ انْطَلَقَ حَتَّى إِذَا اسْتَوَى بِمَاءِ مَغْمَسَ أَمَرَ الفِيلَ فَمَا أَمْكَنَهُ فَلَمَّا أَرَادَ أَنْ يَقْبِلَ عَلَى الكَعْبَةِ قَصَدَ فَمَا أَمْكَنَهُ ثُمَّ أَدْبَرَ فَقَصَدَ فَمَا أَمْكَنَهُ فَأَرْسَلَ اللَّهُ عَلَيْهِمْ طَيْرًا أَبَابِيلَ

Inna abrahata alhabashi arada an yahdima alkabata fa'aadda lidhalika alfeela wajama'an nasa thumma intalaqa hatta 'idha istawa bima'i maghmasa amara alfeela fama 'amkanahu falamma arada an yaqubila 'ala alkabata qasada fama 'amkanahu thumma adbara faqasada fama 'amkanahu fa'arsala allahu 'alayhim tayrana ababeela

Indeed, Abrahah the Abyssinian wanted to demolish the Ka'bah, he prepared an elephant for that and gathered the people then set out. When he reached the water of Muhassab, he ordered the elephant but it could not. Whenever it was directed towards the Ka'bah, it refused to move. Then, Allah sent upon them birds in flocks.

Source: Surah Al-Fil

Dua for Entering the Bathroom

بِسْمِ اللَّهِ اللَّهُمَّ إِنِّي أَعُوذُ بِكَ مِنَ الْخُبْثِ وَالْخَبَائِثِ

Bismillah, Allahumma inni a'udhu bika minal-khubthi wal-khaba'ith.

In the name of Allah, O Allah, I seek refuge with You from all evil and evil-doers.

Source: Sahih Muslim 375

Story of Wisdom:

قَالَ النَّبِيُّ صلى الله عليه وسلم: "لَا يُؤْمِنُ
أَحَدُكُمْ حَتَّى يُحِبَّ لِأَخِيهِ مَا يُحِبُّ لِنَفْسِهِ"

Qala al-nabiyyu salla Allah 'alayhi wa sallam: "La yu'minu ahadukum hatta yuhibba li'akhihi ma yuhibbu linafsihi."

The Prophet (peace be upon him) said, "None of you truly believes until he loves for his brother what he loves for himself."

Source: Sahih Muslim 45

Dua for Exiting the Bathroom

غُفْرَانَكَ

Ghufranaka

I seek Your forgiveness.

Source: Sahih al-Bukhari 6209

Story of Wisdom:

وَقَالَ رَسُولُ اللَّهِ صلى الله عليه وسلم: "إِنَّ
اللَّهَ يُحِبُّ الْعَبْدَ التَّوَّابَ النَّقِيَّ الْخَفِيَّ"

Wa qala rasoolu Allahi salla Allahu alayhi wasalam "Inna Allah la yuhibbu al-abda t-tawwaba an-naqiya al-khafiya

The Messenger of Allah (peace be upon him) said "Verily, Allah loves the servant who is repentant, clean, and concealed.

Source: Sahih Muslim 2742

Dua for Wearing New Clothes

اللَّهُمَّ لَكَ الْحَمْدُ أَنْتَ كَسَوْتَنِيهِ، أَسْأَلُكَ مِنْ خَيْرِهِ وَخَيْرِ
مَا صُنِعَ لَهُ، وَأَعُوذُ بِكَ مِنْ شَرِّهِ وَشَرِّ مَا صُنِعَ لَهُ

Allahumma lakal-hamdu anta kasawtanihi, as'aluka min khairihi wa khairi ma suni'a lahu, wa a'udhu bika min sharrihi wa sharri ma suni'a lahu

O Allah, praise to You for clothing me with this. I ask You for the goodness of it and the goodness for which it was made, and I seek refuge in You from the evil of it and the evil for which it was made.

Source: Sunan Abu Dawood 4020

Story of Wisdom:

كَانَ رَسُولُ اللَّهِ صَلَّى اللهُ عليه وسلّم يُحِبُّ الْفَضْلَ فِي الشَّيْءِ كُلِّهِ

Kana rasoolu Allah salla Allah alayhi wa sallam yuhibbu al-fadla fi al-shay'i kullihi

The Messenger of Allah (peace be upon him) loved to start with the right side in all matters.

Source: Sahih al-Bukhari 5854

Dua for Looking in the Mirror

اللَّهُمَّ أَنْتَ حَسَّنْتَ خَلْقِي فَحَسِّنْ خُلُقِي

Allahumma anta hassanta khalqi fa hassin khuluqi

O Allah, just as You have made my external features beautiful, make my character beautiful as well

Source: Musnad Ahmad 1661

Story of Wisdom:

وَإِذَا خَاطَبَهُمُ الْجَاهِلُونَ قَالُوا سَلَامًا

Wa idha khatabahumu al-jahiloona qaloo salama

And when the ignorant address them, they say, "Peace!"

Source: Quran 25:63

Dua for Leaving the House

بِسْمِ اللَّهِ تَوَكَّلْتُ عَلَى اللَّهِ وَلَا حَوْلَ وَلَا قُوَّةَ إِلَّا بِاللَّهِ

Bismillahi tawakkaltu 'ala Allahi wa la hawla wa la quwwata illa billah.

In the name of Allah, I place my trust in Allah, and there is no might nor power except with Allah.

Source: Sunan Abi Dawud 5095

Story of Wisdom:

عَنْ عَبْدِ اللَّهِ قَالَ قَالَ رَسُولُ اللَّهِ صلى الله عليه وسلم، ‏"‏ يَا مَعْشَرَ الشَّبَابِ مَنِ اسْتَطَاعَ مِنْكُمُ الْبَاءَةَ فَلْيَتَزَوَّجْ، فَإِنَّهُ أَغَضُّ لِلْبَصَرِ وَأَحْصَنُ لِلْفَرْجِ، وَمَنْ لَمْ يَسْتَطِعْ فَعَلَيْهِ بِالصَّوْمِ، فَإِنَّهُ لَهُ وِجَاءٌ ‏"‏.

'An 'Abdillahi qala qala Rasulullahi salla Allahu 'alayhi wa sallam "Ya ma'shara al-shababi mani ista'thaa minkumu al-ba'ata falyatazawwaj, fainnahu aghaddu lil-basari wa ahsanu lil-farji, wa man lam yastati' fa'alyhi bi-sawmi, fainnahu lahu wijaaun."

Narrated Abdullah: The Messenger of Allah (peace be upon him) said: "O young people! Whoever among you can marry, should marry, because it helps him lower his gaze and guard his modesty, and whoever is not able to marry, should fast, as fasting diminishes sexual power."

Source: Sahih al-Bukhari 5066

Dua for Entering the Mosque

اللّٰهُمَّ افْتَحْ لِي أَبْوَابَ رَحْمَتِكَ

Allahumma aftah li abwaba rahmatika

O Allah, open the doors of Your mercy for me.

Source: Sunan Abu Dawud 466

Story of Wisdom:

لَقَدْ كَانَ لَكُمْ فِي رَسُولِ اللَّهِ أُسْوَةٌ حَسَنَةٌ لِّمَنْ كَانَ
يَرْجُو اللَّهَ وَالْيَوْمَ الْآخِرَ وَذَكَرَ اللَّهَ كَثِيرًا

Laqad kana lakum fee rasooli Allahi uswatun hasanatun liman kana yarjoo Allah waalyawma alakhira wathakara Allaha katheera

Indeed in the Messenger of Allah, you have a good example for him who hopes in Allah and the Last Day and remembers Allah much.

Source: Surah Al-Ahzab, 33:21

Dua for Leaving the Mosque

بِسْمِ اللَّهِ وَالصَّلَاةُ وَالسَّلَامُ عَلَىٰ رَسُولِ اللَّهِ

Bismillahi was-salatu was-salamu 'ala Rasulillah

In the name of Allah, and prayers and peace be upon the Messenger of Allah.

Source: Sahih al-Bukhari 3009

Story of Wisdom:

لَا يُكَلِّفُ اللَّهُ نَفْسًا إِلَّا وُسْعَهَا

La yukallifullahu nafsan illa wus'aha

Allah does not burden a soul beyond that it can bear.

Source: Quran 2:286

Dua for Beginning a Journey

اللّهُمَّ أنت الصاحب في السفر، والخليفة في الأهل

Allahumma antas sahibu fis safar, wal khalifatu fil ahli

Oh Allah, You are the Companion in the journey and the Successor over the family.

Source: Sahih Muslim 2697

Story of Wisdom:

قال رسول الله صلّى الله عليه وسلّم:"المسلم من سلم المسلمون من لسانه ويده، والمهاجر من هجر ما نهى الله عنه".

Qala rasool Allahi salla Allah 'alayh wa sallam: "Al muslimu man salima al muslimoona min lisanhi wa yadih, wal muhajiru man hajara ma naha Allah 'anhu".

The Messenger of Allah, peace be upon him, said: "The Muslim is the one from whose tongue and hand the Muslims are safe, and the Emigrant is the one who refrains from what Allah has forbidden."

Source: Sahih al-Bukhari 10

Dua for Protection from Envy

اللّهُمَّ إنّي أعوذ بك من الحسد

Allahumma inni a'udhu bika min al-hasad

O Allah, I seek refuge with You from envy.

Source: Al-Adab Al-Mufrad 273

Story of Wisdom:

قال رسول الله صلّى الله عليه وسلّم: إياكم والحسد، فإن الحسد يأكل الحسنات كما تأكل النار الحطب

Qala rasul allah salla allah 'alayh wa sallam: iyyakum wa al-hasad, fa inna al-hasada ya'kul al-hasanat kama ta'kul al-nar al-hatab

The Prophet Muhammad (peace be upon him) said: "Beware of envy, for envy consumes good deeds just as fire consumes wood."

Source: Sunan Abu Dawood 4903

Dua for Seeking Knowledge

اللّٰهُمَّ انْفَعْنِي بِمَا عَلَّمْتَنِي وَ عَلِّمْنِي مَا يَنْفَعُنِي وَ زِدْنِي عِلْمًا

Allahumma anfa'ni bima 'allamtani wa 'allimni ma yanfa'uni wa zidni 'ilma

O Allah, benefit me from what You have taught me, and teach me what will benefit me, and increase my knowledge.

Source: Jami` at-Tirmidhi 3599

Story of Wisdom:

قال رسول الله صلّى الله عليه وسلّم: ألم يكن لك رجل صالح من إخوانك أو جيرانك فيقولون له: أمكنا أن نقرأ عليك صبيحة كل يوم أو مساء كل ليلة آية من كتاب الله عزّ و جلّ.

Qala rasool Allah salla Allah 'alayh wa sallam: "Alam yakin lak rajul salih min ikhwanik aw jiranik fiquluna lahu: Ummikna an naqra 'alayka sabihah kull yawm aw masa'a kull laylah ayah min kitab Allah 'az wa jal."

The Messenger of Allah, peace be upon him, said, "Don't you have a righteous man among your brothers or neighbors who can recite to you every morning or evening a verse from the Book of Allah, the Almighty and Majestic."

Source: Sahih al-Bukhari 5049

Dua for Good Health

اللّٰهُمَّ إِنِّي أَسْأَلُكَ الْعَافِيَةَ فِي الدُّنْيَا والآخِرَةِ اللّٰهُمَّ إِنِّي أَسْأَلُكَ الْعَفْوَ والْعَافِيَةَ فِي دِينِي ودُنْيَايَ وأَهْلِي ومَالِي

Allahumma inni as'aluka al-'aafiyata fi'd-dunya wa'l-akhirah. Allahumma inni as'aluka al-afwa wa'l-'aafiyata fi dini wa dunyai wa ahli wa mali

Oh Allah, I ask You for well-being in this world and the Hereafter. Oh Allah, I ask Your forgiveness and well-being in my religious and worldly affairs, and for my family and my wealth.

Source: Jami` at-Tirmidhi 3480

Story of Wisdom:

عن أبي هريرة، قال: جاء رجل إلى النبيّ، صلّى الله عليه وسلم، فقال: يا رسول الله، إنّي أصبت جدّة، فأيّ الصّدقة أفضل؟ قال: ماء

'An Abi Hurayra, Qala: Jaa rajulun ila an-Nabi, salla Allahu 'alayhi wa sallam, faqala: Ya Rasul Allah, inni asabtu juda, fa ayyu as-sadaqati afdal? Qala: Ma'

On the authority of Abu Huraira, he said: A man came to the Prophet, peace be upon him, and said: "O Messenger of Allah, I have become very rich, what kind of charity is best?" He (the Prophet) said: Water.

Source: Sunan Ibn Majah 3684

Dua for Forgiveness

اللَّهُمَّ إِنَّكَ عَفُوٌّ تُحِبُّ الْعَفْوَ فَاعْفُ عَنِّي

Allahumma innaka 'afuwwun tuhibbul 'afwa fa'fu 'anni

O Allah, You are Oft-Pardoning and You love pardon, so pardon me.

Source: Sunan al-Tirmidhi 3513

Story of Wisdom:

حدثنا أبو اليمان، قال أخبرنا شعيب، عن الزهري، قال حدثني عبيد الله بن عبد الله، أنّ ابن عباس، قال لما حضر رسول الله صلى الله عليه وسلم وفي بيته عائشة رضي الله عنها وفاطمة رضي الله عنها فقال - أو كأنّه قال - لفاطمة - حين ضمرته - رغبة في الموت اي رسول الله فقال الله اكبر إنّ الموت لسكرات.

Hadathana Abu Al-Yaman, qala akhbarana Shu'ayb, 'an Al-Zuhri, qala hadathani 'Ubayd Allah bin 'Abd Allah, 'anna Ibn 'Abbas, qala lama hadara Rasul Allah salla Allah 'alayh wa sallam al-wafat wa fi baytih 'A'ishah radi Allah 'anha wa Fatimah radi Allah 'anha faqala - aw ka'annahu qala - li Fatimah

17

- hina hadarath - 'araaki raghibatan fi al-mawt ya Rasul Allah faqala Allah Akbar inna lil mawti la sakarat.

Abu Al-Yaman narrated that Shu'ayb told us from Al-Zuhri, that Ubayd Allah bin 'Abd Allah told him, that Ibn 'Abbas said: When the Messenger of Allah (peace and blessings be upon him) was on his death-bed in the house of 'A'ishah (may Allah be pleased with her) and Fatimah (may Allah be pleased with her), he said - or it was as if he said - to Fatimah - when she attended to him - "It seems that you wish for death, O Messenger of Allah." He said: "Allah is the Greatest. Indeed, death has its stupor."

Source: Sahih al-Bukhari 4437

Dua for Guidance

اللّهُمَّ اهدِني فيمن هديت، وعافِني فيمن تولّيت وتَوَلّني فيمن تولّيت

Allahumma ihdini fiman hadayt, wa 'afini fiman 'afayt, wa tawallani fiman tawallayt

Oh Allah, guide me among those whom You have guided, pardon me among those whom You have pardoned, and take me into Your charge among those whom You have taken into Your charge.

Source: Jami' at-Tirmidhi 464

Story of Wisdom:

إذ قال له ربّه أسلم قال أسلمتُ لربّ العالمين

Ith qala lahu rabbuhu aslim qala aslamtu lirabil'alamin

When his Lord said to him, "Submit!" He replied, "I have submitted to the Lord of all the Worlds."

Source: Quran, 2:131

Chapter 2:
Protection through Faith: Daily Duas for Safety and Divine Support

Dua for Protection from Anxiety

اللَّهُمَّ إِنِّي أَعُوذُ بِكَ مِنَ الْهَمِّ وَالْحَزَنِ، وَالْعَجْزِ وَالْكَسَلِ، وَالْبُخْلِ وَالْجُبْنِ، وَضَلَعِ الدَّيْنِ وَغَلَبَةِ الرِّجَالِ

Allahumma inni a'udhu bika min al-hammi wal hazan, wal 'ajzi wal kasal, wal bukhli wal jubn, wa dala'id-dayni wa ghalabatir-rijal.

Oh Allah, I seek refuge in You from anxiety and sorrow, weakness and laziness, miserliness and cowardice, the burden of debts and from being overpowered by men.

Source: Sahih al-Bukhari 6369

Story of Wisdom:

إِذَا أَصَابَتْهُ مُصِيبَةٌ قَالَ إِنَّا لِلَّهِ وَإِنَّا إِلَيْهِ رَاجِعُونَ وَاللَّهُمَّ أُجْرِنِي فِي مُصِيبَتِي أَوْ أَخْلِفْ لِي خَيْرًا مِنْهَا

Idha asabathu museebatun qala inna lillahi wa inna ilayhi raji'un wallahumma ajurni fee museebati wa akhlif li khayran minha

When he was afflicted with a tragedy, he would say, "Verily we belong to Allah and unto Him we shall return. Oh Allah, reward me in my affliction and replace it with something better for me."

Source: Sahih Muslim 918

Dua for Protection of Family

بِسْمِ اللهِ الرَّحْمٰنِ الرَّحِيمِ

اللَّهُمَّ أَصْلِحْ لِي فِي ذُرِّيَّتِي إِنِّي تُبْتُ إِلَيْكَ وَإِنِّي مِنَ الْمُسْلِمِينَ

Bismillāhi r-raḥmāni r-raḥīm

Allāhumma aṣliḥ lī fī durriyyatī innī tubtu ilayka wa innī min al-muslimīn

In the name of Allah, the Most Gracious, the Most Merciful

Oh Allah, make my offspring righteous, I have turned to you and indeed I am of the Muslims.

Source: Qur'an, Surah Al-Ahqaf, 46:15

Story of Wisdom:

عن أبي هريره رضي الله عنه قال: قال رسول الله صلى
الله عليه وسلّم: ,,إذا مات الإنسان انقطع عمله إلا من آل ثالث:
صدقة جارية، أو علم ينتفع به، أو ولد صالح يدعو له``

An abi hurayrah radi Allahu anhu qal: qal rasul Allahi salla Allahu alayhi wa sallam: "Idha mat al-insan inqata'a amaluhu illa min thalath: sadaqah jariyah, 'aw 'ilmun yuntafa' bihi, 'aw waladun salihun yad'ou lahu"

Narrated by Abu Hurairah, may Allah be pleased with him, who said: The Messenger of Allah, peace and blessings be upon him, said: "When a person dies, his deeds are severed except for three things: a continuous charity, knowledge that is benefited from, or a righteous child who prays for him."

Source: Sahih Muslim, 1631

Dua for Protection in Sleep

بِاسْمِكَ اَللَّهُمَّ أَمُوتُ وَأَحْيَا

Bismika allahumma amootu wa ahya

In Your name, O Allah, I die and I live

Source: Sahih Bukhari 6312

Story of Wisdom:

وَهُوَ الَّذِي يَتَوَفَّاكُم بِالَّيْلِ وَيَعْلَمُ مَا جَرَحْتُم بِالنَّهَارِ ثُمَّ يَبْعَثُكُمْ فِيهِ
لِيُقْضَى أَجَلٌ مُّسَمًّى ۖ ثُمَّ إِلَيْهِ مَرْجِعُكُم ثُمَّ يُنَبِّئُكُم بِمَا كُنتُمْ تَعْمَلُونَ

Wa huwa allathee yatawaffakum billayli wayaAAlamu ma jarrahtum bialnnahari thumma yabAAathukum feehi liyuqda ajalun musamman thumma ilayhi marjiAAukum thumma yunabbi-okum bima kuntum taAAmaloon

And it is He who takes your souls by night and knows what you have committed by day. Then He revives you therein that a specified term may be fulfilled. Then to Him will be your return; then He will inform you about what you used to do.

Source: Qur'an 6:60

Dua for Well-being and Health

اللَّهُمَّ إِنِّي أَسْأَلُكَ الْعَافِيَةَ فِي الدُّنْيَا وَالآخِرَةِ اللَّهُمَّ إِنِّي أَسْأَلُكَ الْعَفْوَ
وَالْعَافِيَةَ فِي دِينِي وَدُنْيَايَ وَأَهْلِي وَمَالِي اللَّهُمَّ اسْتُرْ عَوْرَاتِي
وَآمِنْ رَوْعَاتِي اللَّهُمَّ احْفَظْنِي مِنْ بَيْنِ يَدَيَّ وَمِنْ خَلْفِي وَعَنْ يَمِينِي
وَعَنْ شِمَالِي وَمِنْ فَوْقِي وَأَعُوذُ بِعَظَمَتِكَ أَنْ أُغْتَالَ مِنْ تَحْتِي

Allahumma inni as'aluka al-'aafiyata fid-dunya wal-akhirah, Allahumma inni as'aluka al-'afwa wal-'aafiyata fi deeni wa dunyaaya wa ahli wa maali, Allahumma astur 'awraati wa aamin raw'aati, Allahumma ihfadhni min bayni yadayya wa min khalfi wa 'an yameeni wa 'an shimaali wa min fawqi wa a'udhu bi'adhamatika an ughtaala min tahti.

O Allah, I ask You for well-being in this world and in the Hereafter. O Allah, I ask You for pardon and well-being in my religious and worldly affairs, and my family and my property. O Allah, veil my weaknesses and set at ease my dismay. O Allah, preserve me from the front and from behind and on my right and on my left and from above, and I take refuge in Your greatness from being swallowed up from beneath.

Source: Ibn Majah 2:3830

Story of Wisdom:

قَالَ رَسُولُ اللهِ صَلَّى اللهُ عَلَيْهِ وَسَلَّمَ: ,,مَنْ قَالَ حِينَ يُصْبِحُ
وَحِينَ يُمْسِي: رَضِيتُ بِاللهِ رَبًّا وَبِالإِسْلامِ دِينًا وَبِمُحَمَّدٍ صَلَّى
اللهُ عَلَيْهِ وَسَلَّمَ نَبِيًّا، فَأَنَا الزَّعِيمُ لَهُ أَنْ أُقْبِضَهُ يَوْمَ الْقِيَامَةِ،،

Qala rasulullahi sallallahu 'alayhi wa sallam: "Man qala hina yusbihu wa hina yumsi: radiitu billahi rabban wa bil-islami dinan wa bi Muhammadin sallallahu 'alayhi wa sallam nabiyyan, fa ana al-zaeem lahu an aqbidahu yawm al-qiyamah."

The Messenger of Allah, peace and blessings be upon him, said, "Whoever says when he morning and when he evening, 'I am pleased with Allah as my Lord, with Islam as my religion, and with Muhammad, peace and blessings be upon him, as my Prophet,' then I am the guarantor for him that I will take him by his hand on the Day of Resurrection."

Source: Jami` at-Tirmidhi 3388

Dua for Protection from Evil Eye

بِسْمِ اللهِ الَّذِي لَا يَضُرُّ مَعَ اسْمِهِ شَيْءٌ فِي الْأَرْضِ
وَلَا فِي السَّمَاءِ وَهُوَ السَّمِيعُ الْعَلِيمُ

Bismillah alladhee la yadurru ma' ismihi shay'un fil ardi wa la fis samaa' wa huwa as-samee' ul 'aleem

In the name of Allah, with whose name nothing can harm on Earth nor in the Heavens, and He is the All-Hearing, All-Knowing.

Source: At-Tirmidhi 3388

Story of Wisdom:

قال رسول الله صلّى الله عليه وسلّم : إن الله يغار
وغيرة الله أن يأتي المرء ما حرم الله عليه ،

Qaal rasoollullahi sallallahu alaihi wasallam: Inna Allaha yaghar, waghayratu Allahi an yatiy almaru ma harrama Allahu 'alayh

The Messenger of Allah (peace be upon him) said: "Indeed, Allah is Jealous, and the jealousy of Allah is that a believer should do what Allah has forbidden."

Source: Sahih al-Bukhari 6120

Dua for Recovery from Illness

اللّهَمّ رَبّ النّاس، أذهب البأس، اشفِ أنتَ الشّافي،
لا شافي إلّا أنتَ، شفاءً لا يغادر سقمًا

Allahumma Rabban-nas, adhhibil-ba'sa, ishfi Anta Ash-Shafi, la shafiya illa Anta, shifa'an la yughadiru saqama

O Allah, the Lord of mankind, remove the illness, cure (the patient), for You are the Healer. None brings about healing but You; a healing that will leave behind no ailment.

Source: Sahih al-Bukhari 5743, Sahih Muslim 2191

Story of Wisdom:

قال النبيّ صلّى الله عليه و سلّم: ,,ما أصاب أحدٍ هماً و لا
حزن فقال: اللّهمَّ إنّي عبدك، وابن عبدك، وابن أمتك، ناصيتي
بيدك، ماضٍ فيّ حكمك، عدل في قضائك، أسألك لكل اسم هو
بيدك، سمّيت به نفسك، أو أنزلته في كتابك، و أو علمته أحداً
من خلقك، أو استأثرت به في علم الغيب عندك، أن تجعل
القرآن العظيم ربيع قلبي، ونور صدري، وجلاء حزني،
وذهاب همي، إلا أذهب الله همَّه وحزنه، وأبدله مكانه فرجاً".

Qala an-nabiyyu Muhammadun salla Allahu 'alayhi wa sallam: "Ma asaba ahadan hamun wala huznun faqala: Allahumma inni 'abduka, wa ibnu 'abdika, wa ibnu amatika, nasiyati biyadika, madin fi hukmika, 'adlun fi qada'ika, as'aluka bikulli ismin huwa laka, sammayta bihi nafsaka, aw anzaltahu fi kitabika, aw 'allamtahu ahadan min khalqika, aw ista'tharta bihi fi 'ilm al-ghaybi 'indaka, an taj'al al-Qur'an al-'Adheema rabi'a qalbi, wa noora sadri, wa jalaa'a huzni, wa dhahaba hami, illa adhhaba Allahu hamahu wa huznahu, wa abdalah makanahu farajan."

The Prophet Muhammad (peace and blessings of Allah be upon him) said: "No one is stricken with anxiety or sorrow, and says: 'O Allah, I am Your servant, son of Your servant, son of Your maidservant. My forelock is in Your hand, Your command over me is forever executed and Your decree over me is just. I ask You by every Name belonging to You which You named Yourself with, or revealed in Your Book, or You taught to any of Your creation, or You have preserved in the knowledge of the unseen with You, that You make the Qur'an the life of my heart and the light of my chest, and a departure for my sorrow and a release for my anxiety,' but Allah will take away his sorrow and grief, and give him in their stead joy."

Source: Ahmad 1/391.

Dua for Steadfastness in Faith

اللّهمَّ يا مُقلّبَ القلُوبِ ثبّت قلبي عَلى دينكَ

Allahumma ya muqallibal-qulubi, thabbit qalbi 'ala deenika

Oh Allah, you who turns hearts, make my heart steadfast in Your religion.

Source: Sunan ibn Majah, Nr. 3834

Story of Wisdom:

وقد كان رسول الله صلى الله عليه وسلم يعظ أصحابه قائلا: ,,ألا إنّ القلوب بين أصبعين من أصابع الله، يقلبها فيك شيئاء"

Wa qad kana rasul Allah salla Allah alayh wa sallam ya'iz ashabahu qa'ila: "Ala inna alquluba bayna usba'ayn min asabi' Allah, yaqallibaha kayf yasha."

Indeed, the Messenger of Allah, peace be upon him, used to advise his companions by saying, "Indeed, the hearts are between two fingers of the fingers of Allah, He turns them as He wills."

Source: Sahih Muslim, 2654

Dua for Safety in Travel

بِسْمِ اللهِ الَّذِي لَا يَضُرُّ مَعَ اسْمِهِ شَيْءٌ فِي الْأَرْضِ وَلَا فِي السَّمَاءِ وَهُوَ السَّمِيعُ الْعَلِيمُ

Bismillahillazi La Yadurru Ma'asmihi Shay'un Filardi Wala Fis-sama'i Wa Huwas-sami'ul 'Alim

In the name of Allah with whose name nothing can harm on Earth nor in the Heavens, and He is the All-Hearing, the All-Knowing.

Source: Abu Dawood, Tirmidhi

Story of Wisdom:

إذ قال له ربّه أسلم قال أسلمت لربّ العالمين

Idh qala lahu rabbuhu aslim qala aslamtu lirabbi alAAalameena

When his Lord said to him, "Submit (i.e. in Islam)," he said "I have submitted myself (as a Muslim) to the Lord of the 'Alamin (mankind, jinn and all that exists)."

Source: Qur'an Surah Al-Baqarah (2:131)

Dua for Success and Prosperity

اللهُمَّ لَكَ أَسْلَمْتُ، وبِكَ آمَنتُ، وعَلَيكَ تَوَكَّلْتُ، وإِلَيكَ أَنَبْتُ،
وبِكَ خاصَمتُ، اللّهُمَّ إِنِّي أَعوذُ بِعِزَّتِكَ لا إِلهَ إلّا أَنتَ أَن
تُضِلَّنِي، أَنتَ الحَيّ الّذي لا يَموتُ، والجِنّ والإنسُ يَموتونَ

Allahumma laka aslamtu, wa bika aamantu, wa 'alaika tawakkaltu, wa ilayka anabtu, wa bika khasamtu, Allahumma inni a'udhu bi'izzatika la ilaha illa anta an tudhillani, anta al-hayy alladhee la yamoot, wa al-jinn wa al-ins yamootoon

O Allah, To You I have submitted, and in You do I believe, and in You I put my trust, To You do I turn, and for You I argued. O Allah, I seek refuge with Your might, there is no god but You, lest I go astray. You are the Ever-living who never dies, while the jinn and the humans die.

Source: Sahih Muslim 2717

Story of Wisdom:

لَمّا ضاقَت على النَبيِّ صلى الله عليه وسلَّم الأحزابَ قالَ: ,,اللّهُمَّ
مُنزِلَ الكِتابَ، سَريعَ الحِسابَ، اهزِمِ الأحزابَ، اللّهُمَّ اهزِمهُم وزَلزِلهُم"

Lamma daaqat 'ala annabiyyi salla Allahu 'alayhi wa sallam al-ahzab qala: "Allahumma munzil alkitaab, saree' alhisaab, ihzim al-ahzab, Allahumma ihzimhum wazalzilhum"

When the Prophet (peace and blessings be upon him) was severely tested by the Confederates, he said: "O Allah, Revealer of the Book, Swift at the Reckoning, defeat the Confederates. O Allah, defeat them and shake them."

Source: Sahih al-Bukhari 4114

Dua for Protection from Satan

بِسْمِ اللهِ الرَّحْمٰنِ الرَّحيمِ

الَّلهُمَّ إِنِّي أَعوذُ بِكَ مِنْ الشَّرِّ النَّفْثاتِ في العُقَدِ

وَمِنْ شَرِّ حاسِدٍ إذا حَسَدَ

وَمِنْ شَرِّ ذِي عَيْنٍ

3ismi Allahi arrahmani arraheem

25

Allahumma inni a'udhu bika min sharri al-nafathati fi al-'uqad

wa min sharri hasidin idha hasad

wa min sharri kulli dhi'ayn

In the name of Allah, the Most Gracious, the Most Merciful

O Allah, I seek refuge with You from the evil of those who blow on knots,

and from the evil of a envier when he envies,

and from the evil of every possessor of an evil eye.

Source: Al-Falaq 113:1-5

Story of Wisdom:

وَإِذْ قَالَ مُوسَىٰ لِفَتَاهُ لَا أَبْرَحُ حَتَّىٰ أَبْلُغَ مَجْمَعَ الْبَحْرَيْنِ أَوْ أَمْضِيَ حُقُبًا

Wa-idh qala Musa lifatahu la abrahu hatta ablugha majma' al-bahrayni aw amdhiya huquba

And [recall] when Moses said to his servant, "I will not cease [traveling] until I reach the junction of the two seas or continue for a long period."

Source: Al-Kahf 18:60

Dua for Ease in Difficulties

اللَّهُمَّ لَا سَهْلَ إِلَّا مَا جَعَلْتَهُ سَهْلًا، وَأَنْتَ تَجْعَلُ الْحَزْنَ إِذَا شِئْتَ سَهْلًا

Allahumma la sahla illa ma ja'altahu sahla, wa 'anta taj-alul hazna idha shi'ta sahla

Oh Allah, there is no ease except in what You have made easy, and You make the difficulty, if You wish, easy.

Source: Sahih al-Bukhari 6366

Story of Wisdom:

قال رسول الله صلى الله عليه وسلم: إذا أراد الله بعبده
الخير عجل له العقوبة في الدنيا. وإذا أراد الله بعبده
الشر أمسك عنه بذنبه حتى يواجهه به يوم القيامة

Qaal rasul Allahi salla Allahi 'alayhi wa sallam: 'Idha 'arad Allahu bi 'abdih al-khair 'ajjil lahu al-uqubah fi al-dunya. Wa 'idha 'arad Allahu bi 'abdihi al-sharr 'amsak 'anhu bi dhanbih hatta yuwajihahu bihi yawm al-qiyamah

Prophet Muhammad (peace be upon him) said: "When Allah intends good for His servant, He hastens the punishment for him in this world. And when Allah intends evil for His servant, He withholds the punishment for his sin until He confronts him with it on the Day of Judgment."

Source: Sahih al-Bukhari 5648

BONUS

Dear Reader,

We thank you for supporting us in carrying the message of Allah to the world.

We regularly have further updates on other projects and would be happy if you subscribe to our newsletter:

A positive surprise and our thanks are waiting for you.

Chapter 3:
Strengthening Faith: Duas for Patience and Spirituality

Dua for Increased Faith

اَللّٰهُمَّ يَا مُقَلِّبَ الْقُلُوبِ ثَبِّتْ قَلْبِي عَلَى دِينِكَ

Allahumma Ya Muqallib al-Quloob, thabbit qalbi 'ala deenika

O Allah, O Turner of the hearts, make my heart firm in Your religion.

Source: Jami` at-Tirmidhi 2140

Story of Wisdom:

قَالَ رَسُولُ اللّٰهِ صَلَّى اللّٰه عليه و سلم، إِنَّ الدُّنْيَا مَلْعُونَةٌ مَلْعُونٌ مَا فِيهَا إِلَّا ذِكْرُ اللّٰهِ وَمَا وَالَاهُ وَعَالِمٌ أَوْ مُتَعَلِّمٌ

Qala rasool Allahi salla Allah alaihi wa sallam, "Ad-dunya mal'oona, mal'oonun ma feeha illa dhikr Allah wa ma waalaahu wa 'aalimun aw muta'allim."

The Messenger of Allah, peace be upon him, said, "The world is cursed; cursed is what it contains, except for the remembrance of Allah, what is conducive to that, a scholar, or a student.

Source: Sunan Ibn Majah 4112

Dua for Gratitude and Contentment

اَللّٰهُمَّ إِنِّي أَعُوذُ بِكَ مِنْ زَوَالِ نِعْمَتِكَ، وَتَحَوُّلِ عَافِيَتِكَ، وَفُجَاءَةِ نِقْمَتِكَ، وَجَمِيعِ سَخَطِكَ

Allahumma inni a'udhu bika min zawali ni'matika, wa tahawwuli 'afiyatika, wa fuja'ati niqmatika, wa jami'i sakhatika

Oh Allah, I seek refuge in You from the decline of Your blessings, the removal of my state of wellbeing, the sudden onset of Your punishment and from all that displeases You.

Source: Sahih Muslim 2739

Story of Wisdom:

وَإِذْ تَأَذَّنَ رَبُّكُمْ لَئِن شَكَرْتُمْ لَأَزِيدَنَّكُمْ وَلَئِن كَفَرْتُمْ إِنَّ عَذَابِي لَشَدِيدٌ

Wa idh ta'adhdhana rabbukum la'in shakartum la'azidannakum wa la'in kafartum inna 'adhabi lashadeed

And remember when Your Lord proclaimed, 'If you are grateful, I will surely increase you [in favor]; but if you deny, indeed, My punishment is severe.'

Source: Holy Qur'an 14:7

Dua for Closer Bond with Allah

اللَّهُمَّ إِنِّي أَسْأَلُكَ حُبَّكَ وَحُبَّ مَن يُحِبُّكَ وَحُبَّ كُلِّ عَمَلٍ يُقَرِّبُنِي إِلَى حُبِّكَ

Allahumma inni as'aluka hubbaka, wa hubba may yuhibbuka, wa hubba kulli 'amalin yuqarribuni ila hubbika

Oh Allah, I ask You for Your love and the love of those who love You, and for the love of every action that can bring me closer to Your love.

Source: Musnad Ahmad 16365

Story of Wisdom:

وَلَقَدْ خَلَقْنَا الْإِنسَانَ وَنَعْلَمُ مَا تُوَسْوِسُ بِهِ نَفْسُهُ وَنَحْنُ أَقْرَبُ إِلَيْهِ مِنْ حَبْلِ الْوَرِيدِ

Wa laqad khalaqna al-insana wa na'lamu ma tuwaswisu bihi nafsuhu, wa nahnu aqrabu ilayhi min habli al-wariid

And certainly, We created man and We are closer to him than his life vein.

Source: Qur'an 50:16

Dua for Forgiveness of Sins

اللّهُمَّ إِنِّي ظَلَمْتُ نَفْسِي ظُلْمًا كَثِيرًا وَلَا يَغْفِرُ الذُّنُوبَ إِلَّا أَنْتَ
فَاغْفِرْ لِي مَغْفِرَةً مِنْ عِنْدِكَ وَارْحَمْنِي إِنَّكَ أَنْتَ الْغَفُورُ الرَّحِيمُ

Allahumma inni zalamtu nafsi zulman kathiran wa la yaghfiru dh-dhunuba illa anta, faghfir li maghfiratan min 'indika war-hamni, innaka antal Ghafur-ur Rahim.

Oh Allah, I have greatly wronged myself, and no one forgives sins but You. So grant me forgiveness and have mercy on me. Surely, You are the Most Forgiving, Most Merciful.

Source: Sahih Bukhari 834

Story of Wisdom:

كَانَ فِيمَنْ كَانَ قَبْلَكُمْ رَجُلٌ قَتَلَ تِسْعَةً وَتِسْعِينَ نَفْسًا فَأَسَلَ
عَنْ أَعْلَمِ النَّاسِ فَدُلَّ عَلَى رَاهِبٍ فَأَتَاهُ فَقَالَ إِنِّي قَتَلْتُ تِسْعَةً
وَتِسْعِينَ نَفْسًا فَهَلْ لِي تَوْبَةٌ فَقَالَ لَا فَقَتَلَهُ فَكَمَّلَ بِهِ مِائَةً

Kana feeman kana qablakum rajulun qatala tis'atan wa tis'eena nafsan fas'ala 'an a'alam alnnasi fadulliya 'ala rahibin fa'atahu faqala innee qataltu tis'atan wa tis'eena nafsan fahal li tawbatun faqala la faqatalahu fakamala bihi mi'atan.

There was, before your time, a man who had killed 99 people. Then he inquired about the most learned person and was directed to a monk. He told him that he had killed 99 people and asked if there was any chance for repentance for him. The monk said 'No', so he killed him as well, completing 100 murders.

Source: Sahih Muslim 2766

Dua for Protection from Doubt

اللّهُمَّ إِنِّي أَعُوذُ بِكَ مِنَ الشُّبُهَاتِ وَالرَّيْبِ

Allahumma inni a'udhu bika min ash-shubuhati wa ar-rayb

Oh Allah, I seek refuge with You from doubts and suspicions.

Source: Jami` at-Tirmidhi 3604

Story of Wisdom:

قَالَ رَجُلٌ لِلنَّبِيِّ صَلَّى اللهُ عَليهِ وَ سَلَّمَ اي رَسُولَ اللَّهِ مَا النَّجَاةُ قَالَ
أَمْسِكْ عَلَيْكَ لِسَانَكَ وَلْيَسَعْكَ بَيْتُكَ وَابْكِ عَلَى خَطِيئَتِكَ

Qala rajulun lin-nabiyyi salla Allahu 'alayhi wa sallam ya rasul Allah ma an-najatu? Qala "amsik 'alayka lisanaka wa lyasa'ka baytuka wa ibki 'ala khati'atika"

A man said to the Prophet, peace be upon him, "O Messenger of Allah, what is salvation?" He replied, "Control your tongue, let your house be enough for you, and weep for your sins."

Source: Sunan Ibn Majah 3979

Dua for Acceptance of Supplication

اللَّهُمَّ إِنِّي أسألك الهدى والتقى والعفاف والغنى

Allahummah inni as'aluka al-huda wa at-tuqa wa al-'afafa wa al-ghina

Oh Allah, I ask You for guidance, piety, chastity, and independence.

Source: Sahih Muslim 1051

Story of Wisdom:

عَنْ أَبِي هُرَيْرَةَ، قَالَ قَالَ رَسُولُ اللَّهِ صَلَّى اللهُ عَليهِ وَ سَلَّمَ] ,[يَقُولُ
اللَّهُ تَعَالَى أَنَا عِنْدَ ظَنِّ عَبْدِي بِي وَأَنَا مَعَهُ إِذَا ذَكَرَنِي فَإِنْ ذَكَرَنِي
فِي نَفْسِهِ ذَكَرْتُهُ فِي نَفْسِي وَإِنْ ذَكَرَنِي فِي مَلَأٍ ذَكَرْتُهُ فِي مَلَأٍ
خَيْرٍ مِنْهُمْ وَإِنْ تَقَرَّبَ إِلَيَّ بِشِبْرٍ تَقَرَّبْتُ إِلَيْهِ ذِرَاعًا وَإِنْ تَقَرَّبَ
إِلَيَّ ذِرَاعًا تَقَرَّبْتُ إِلَيْهِ بَاعًا وَإِنْ أَتَانِي يَمْشِي أَتَيْتُهُ هَرْوَلَةً[٢٢]

'An Abi Hurayrah, qala qala Rasulullahi Sallallahu 'alayhi wa sallam "Yaquolu Allahu ta'ala Ana 'inda dhanni 'abdi bi wa Ana ma'ahu idha dhakarani fa'in dhakarani fi nafsihi dhakartuhu fi nafsi wa'in dhakarani fi mal'in dhakartuhu fi mal'in khayrin minhum wa'in taqarraba ilayya bi shibrin taqarrabtu ilayhi dhira'an wa'in taqarraba ilayya dhira'an taqarrabtu ilayhi ba'an wa'in atani yamshi ataytuhu harwala."

From Abu Huraira, he said, the Messenger of Allah, peace and blessings be upon him, said: "Allah the Exalted says: 'I am as My servant thinks of Me, and I am with him when he mentions Me. If he mentions Me within himself, I mention him within Myself; and if he mentions Me in an assembly, I mention him in an assembly better than it. If he draws near to Me a hand's span, I draw near to him an arm's length; and if he draws near to Me an arm's length, I draw near to him a fathom's length. And if he comes to Me walking, I go to him running.'"

Source: Sahih al-Bukhari 6856 and Sahih Muslim 2675

Dua for Guidance and Wisdom

اللّهُمَّ إِنِّي أَسْأَلُكَ فِعْـلَ الْخَيْـرَاتِ، وَتَرْكَ الْمُنْكَرَاتِ،
وَحُـبَّ الْمَسَاكِينِ، وَأَنْ تَغْـفِرَ لِي، وَتَرْحَـمَـنِي، وَإِذَا أَرَدْتَـ
بِعِبَادِكَ فِتْنَةً، فَتَوَفَّنِي إِلَيْكَ غَيْـرَ مَفْتُونٍ

Allahumma inni as'aluka fa'la al-khayrati, wa tark al-munkarati, wa hubb al-masakin, wa an taghfira li, wa tarhamani, wa idha aradta bi'ibadika fitnatan, fa tawaffani ilayka ghaira maftoon

Oh Allah, I ask You to enable me to do good deeds, avoid evil deeds, love the poor, and to forgive me and show mercy to me. And if You wish a trial for Your servants, take me to You without being subjected to the trial.

Source: Sahih al-Bukhari 6369

Story of Wisdom:

كان رجل يمشي في طريق فرأى غصن شوك في
الطريق، فأخذه، فشكر اللهُ له فغفر له

Kana rajul yamshi fi tariq fara'a ghusn shawk fi al-tariq fa'akhadhahu, fashakara Allahu lahu faghafar lahu

A man was walking on a road and saw a thorny branch on the road, so he took it. So, Allah thanked him and forgave him.

Source: Sahih al-Bukhari 6614

Dua for Love of Good Deeds

اللَّهُمَّ حَبِّبْ إِلَيَّ فِيهِ الْإِحْسَانَ، وَكَرِّهْ فِيهِ الْفُسُوقَ وَالْعِصْيَانَ، وَحَرِّمْ
عَلَيَّ فِيهِ السَّخَطَ وَالنِّيرَانَ، بِعَوْنِكَ يَا غِيَاثَ الْمُسْتَغِيثِينَ

Allahumma habbib ilaya fihel-ihsana, wa karrih fihi al-fusuqa wal-'isyan, wa harrim 'alayya fihi as-sakhata wan-niran, bi-'awnika ya ghiathal-mustagheethin.

Oh Allah, make me love goodness during it, and make me detest corruption and disobedience, and forbid me from incurring Your wrath and the fire, with Your aid, O the aide of those who seek assistance.

Source: Sahih Ibn Hibban

Story of Wisdom:

عَنِ النَّبِيِّ صَلَّى اللهُ عَلَيْهِ وسلم قَالَ, إِنَّ "كُلَّ سُلَامَى مِنَ النَّاسِ عَلَيْهِ
صَدَقَةٌ كُلَّ يَوْمٍ تَطْلُعُ فِيهِ الشَّمْسُ تَعْدِلُ بَيْنَ الِاثْنَيْنِ صَدَقَةٌ وَتُعِينُ
الرَّجُلَ فِي دَابَّتِهِ فَتَحْمِلُهُ عَلَيْهَا أَوْ تَرْفَعُ لَهُ عَلَيْهَا مَتَاعَهُ صَدَقَةٌ"

Anin-nabiyyi salla Allahu 'alayhi wa sallam qala "kullu sulama minan-nasi 'alayhi sadaqatun kulla yawmin tatlu'u fihish-shamsu ta'dilu baynal-ithnayni sadaqatun wa tu'eenu ar-rajula fid-dabatihi fatahmiluhu 'alayha aw tarfa'u lahu 'alayha mata'ahu sadaqatun".

The Prophet (peace and blessings of Allah be upon him) said: "Every joint of a person must perform a charity each day that the sun rises: to judge justly between two people is a charity; to help a man with his mount, lifting him onto it or hoisting up his belongings onto it, is a charity."

Source: Sahih al-Bukhari 2827 & Sahih Muslim 1009

Dua for Protection from Misguidance

اللَّهُمَّ إِنِّي أَعُوذُ بِكَ مِنْ ضَلَالِ الْفِتَنِ، وَأَعُوذُ بِكَ مِنْ شُرُورِ النَّفْسِ،
وَأَعُوذُ بِكَ مِنَ الْهَوَى وَالشَّهَوَاتِ. اللَّهُمَّ اهْدِنِي فِيمَنْ هَدَيْتَ، وَعَافِنِي
فِيمَنْ عَافَيْتَ، وَتَوَلَّنِي فِيمَنْ تَوَلَّيْتَ، وَبَارِكْ لِي فِيمَا أَعْطَيْتَ،
وَقِنِي شَرَّ مَا قَضَيْتَ، فَإِنَّكَ تَقْضِي وَلَا يُقْضَى عَلَيْكَ، وَإِنَّهُ لَا
يَذِلُّ مَنْ وَالَيْتَ، وَلَا يَعِزُّ مَنْ عَادَيْتَ، تَبَارَكْتَ رَبَّنَا وَتَعَالَيْتَ.

Allahumma inni a'udhu bika min dalal al-fitn, wa a'udhu bika min shurur al-nafs, wa a'udhu bika min al-hawa wa al-shahawat. Allahumma ihdini fi man

hadayt, wa ʿafini fi man ʿafayt, wa tawallani fi man tawallayt, wa barik li fi ma
aʿtayt, wa qini sharra ma qadayt, fa innaka taqdi wa la yuqda ʿalayk, wa innahu
la yadhillu man walayt, wa la yaʿizzu man ʿadayt, tabarakta rabbana wa taʿalayt.

Oh Allah, I seek Your refuge from the misguidance of trials, and I seek Your
refuge from the evils of the self, and I seek Your refuge from desires and
passions. Oh Allah, guide me among those whom You have guided, grant
me health among those whom You have granted health, take me as a friend
among those whom You have taken as friends, bless me in what You have
given, and guard me from the evil of what You have decreed, for indeed You
decree and none can decree upon You. Indeed, he is not humiliated whom
You have befriended, and he is not honored who is Your enemy. Blessed are
You, our Lord, and exalted.

Source: Sahih Muslim 2716

Story of Wisdom:

عن أبي هريرة، عن النبي صلّى الله عليه وسلم قال: ‏‏إن الله
يقول: من عادى لي ولياً فقد آذنته بالحرب، وما تقرب إلي
بشيء أحب إلي مما افترضت عليه، وما يزال عبدي يتقرب إلي
بالنوافل حتى أحبه، فإذا أحببته كنت سمعه الذي يسمع به،
وبصره الذي يبصر به، ويده التي يبطش بها، ورجله التي
يمشي بها، وإن سألني لأعطينه، ولئن استعاذني لأعيذنّه‏‏

ʿan abi hurayra, ʿan al-nabiyyi salla allah ʿalayh wa sallam qal: "inna allah yaqulu:
min ʿada li waliyyan faqad ādhanthu bil-harb, wa ma taqarraba ilayya ʿabdi bi
shayin ahabbu ilayya mimma iftaraḍtu ʿalayh, wa ma yazalu ʿabdi yataqarrabu
ilayya bil-nawāfil ḥatta uḥibbah, fa'idha aḥbabtuhu kuntu samʿahu alladhi
yasmaʿu bih, wa baṣarah alladhi yubaṣiru bih, wa yadahu allati yabṭishu bihā,
wa rijlah allati yamshi bihā, wa in saʿalani la'uʿṭiannah, wa la'in istaʿādhanī
la'uʿīdannah"

From Abu Huraira, the Prophet, peace be upon him, said: "Indeed, Allah says:
'Whoever shows enmity to a friend of Mine, then I have declared war against
him. My servant does not draw close to Me with anything more beloved to
Me than the religious duties I have obligated upon him. And My servant
continues to draw close to me with optional acts so that I shall love him.
When I love him, I am his hearing with which he hears, his seeing with which
he sees, his hand with which he strikes, and his foot with which he walks.
Were he to ask [something] of Me, I would surely give it to him, and were he
to seek refuge with Me, I would surely grant him refuge.'"

Source: Sahih al-Bukhari 6502

Dua for Light in Heart and Soul

اللّٰهُمَّ اجعل في قلبي نورا، وفي لساني نورا، وفي سمعي نورا، وفي
بصري نورا، ومن فوقي نورا، ومن تحتي نورا، وعن يميني نورا،
وعن شمالي نورا، ومن أمامي نورا، ومن خلفي نورا. اللّٰهُمَّ اجعل لي نورا

Allahumma-ja'al fi qalbi nooran, wa fi lisani nooran, wa fi sam'i nooran, wa
fi basari nooran, wa min fawqi nooran, wa min tahti nooran, wa an yameeni
nooran, wa an shimali nooran, wa min amami nooran, wa min khalfi nooran.
Allahumma i'j-al li nooran

Oh Allah, place light in my heart, and on my tongue light, and in my ears
light, and in my sight light, and above me light, and below me light, and to my
right light, and to my left light, and before me light and behind me light. Oh
Allah, grant me light.

Source: Sahih Muslim 763

Story of Wisdom:

وَكَذَلِكَ جَعَلْنَاكُمْ أُمَّةً وَسَطًا لِتَكُونُوا شُهَدَاءَ عَلَى
النَّاسِ وَيَكُونَ الرَّسُولُ عَلَيْكُمْ شَهِيدًا

Wa kadhalika ja'alnakum ummatan wasatan litakoonoo shuhadaa'a ala an-nasi
wa yakoonar-rasoolu 'alaykum shaheeda

And thus we have made you a moderate community that you will be
witnesses over the people and the Messenger will be a witness over you.

Source: Qur'an 2:143

Dua for Purity of Intent

اللّٰهُمَّ إِني أسألك العفو والعافية في الدنيا والآخرة، اللّٰهُمَّ إِني
أسألك العفو والعافية في ديني ودنياي وأهلي ومالي، اللّٰهُمَّ استر
عوراتي وآمن روعاتي واحفظني من بين يدي ومن خلفي وعن
يميني وعن شمالي، ومن فوقي، وأعوذ بعظمتك أن أغتال من تحتي

Allahumma inni as'alukal-'afwa wal-'afiyata fid-dunya wal-akhirah,
Allahumma inni as'alukal-'afwa wal-'afiyata fi dini wa dunyaya wa ahli wa
mali, Allahumma-stur 'awrati wa amin raw'ati wahfazni min bayni yadayya wa
min khalfi wa 'an yamini wa 'an shimali wa min fawqi, wa a'udhu bi'adhamatika
an ughtala min tahti

36

O Allah, I ask You for forgiveness and well-being in this world and the next. O Allah, I ask You for forgiveness and well-being in my religious and my worldly affairs. O Allah, conceal my faults, calm my fears, and protect me from before me and behind me, from my right and my left, and from above me, and I take refuge in Your greatness from being struck down from beneath me.

Source: Al-Adab Al-Mufrad 708, Sahih

Story of Wisdom:

اذا رأى أحدكم من نفسه أو ماله أو من أخيه ما يعجبه
فليدع له بالبركة، فإنّ العين حق

Idha raa ahadukum min nafsihi aw malihi aw min akhihi ma yu'jibuh falyad' lahu bil barakah, fa innal 'ayna haqq

When one of you sees from himself or his wealth or from his brother what he likes, he should invoke blessings for it, for indeed the evil eye is real.

Source: Jami` at-Tirmidhi 3412, Sahih.

Dua for Righteous Actions

اللّهُمّ إِنّي أَعُوذُ بِكَ مِنَ الْمَأْثَمِ وَالْمَغْرَمِ

Allahumma inni a'udhu bika minal-ma'thami wal-maghrami

O Allah, I seek refuge in You from sinning and from being in debt.

Source: Sahih al-Bukhari 832

Story of Wisdom:

قَالَ رَسُولُ اللّهِ صَلّى اللّهِ عَلَيْهِ وَسَلّمَ الدّنْيَا
مَتَاعٌ، وَخَيْرُ مَتَاعِهَا الْمَرْأَةُ الصّالِحَةُ

Qala rasulullahi salla Allahu alayhi wa sallam "ad-dunya mata'un, wa khayru mata'iha al-mar'atu as-salihatu"

The Messenger of Allah (peace be upon him) said, "The world is a provision, and the best provision of the world is a righteous woman."

Source: Sahih Muslim 1467

Chapter 4:
Health and Harmony: Duas for Physical and Spiritual Well-being

Dua for Good Health

اللّٰهُمَّ إِنِّي أَعُوذُ بِكَ مِنَ الْبَرَصِ، وَالْجُنُونِ، وَمِنَ الْجُذَامِ، وَمِنْ سَيِّئِ الْأَسْقَامِ

Allahumma inni a'udhu bika minal-barasi, wal-junooni, wal-juthaami, wa min sayyil-asqaami

Oh Allah, I seek Your refuge from leprosy, insanity, elephantiasis, and from all serious illness.

Source: Sahih al-Bukhari 6368

Story of Wisdom:

وَلَقَدْ أَرْسَلْنَا نُوحًا إِلَىٰ قَوْمِهِ فَلَبِثَ فِيهِمْ أَلْفَ سَنَةٍ إِلَّا خَمْسِينَ عَامًا فَأَخَذَهُمُ الطُّوفَانُ وَهُمْ ظَالِمُونَ

Wa laqad arsalna Nuhan ila qawmihi fala bitha feehim alfa sanatin illa khamsina aaman fa'akhadahumu alttufanu wahum zhalimoon

Indeed, We sent Noah to his people, and he stayed among them a thousand years minus fifty years, and the flood seized them while they were wrongdoers.

Source: Qur'an 29:14

Dua for Healing from Illness

اللّٰهُمَّ رَبَّ النَّاسِ أَذْهِبِ الْبَأْسَ اشْفِ أَنْتَ الشَّافِي لَا شِفَاءَ إِلَّا شِفَاؤُكَ شِفَاءً لَا يُغَادِرُ سَقَمًا

Allahumma Rabban-nas, adhhibil-bas, ishfi Anta Shafi, la shifa'a illa shifa'uka, shifaan la yughadiru saqaman.

38

O Allah, Lord of mankind, remove the affliction and send down cure and healing, for no one can cure but You; so cure in such a way that no ailment is left.

Source: Sahih Al-Bukhari 5743, Sahih Muslim 2191

Story of Wisdom:

قَالَ رَسُوْلُ اللهِ صَلَّى اللهُ عَلَيهِ وسلم: إِذَا مَرِضَ الْعَبْدُ
أَوْ سَافَرَ كُتِبَ لَهُ مِثْلُ مَا كَانَ يَعْمَلُ مُقِيمًا صَحِيحًا

Qala rasool Allahi salla Allah alayhi wa sallam: Idha maridha al-'abd aw safara kutiba lahu mithlu ma kana ya'malu muqiman sahihan.

The Messenger of Allah (peace and blessings be upon him) said: "When a servant (of Allah) falls ill or travels, the same reward is recorded for him as what he would have achieved if he had been healthy and at home."

Source: Sahih Bukhari 2996

Dua for Emotional Stability

رَبِّ اشْرَحْ لِي صَدْرِي وَيَسِّرْ لِي أَمْرِي وَاحْلُلْ
عُقْدَةً مِّنْ لِسَانِي يَفْقَهُ وَ قَوْلِي

Rabbi ishrah li sadri wa yassir li amri wah lul 'uqdatan min lisani yafqahu qawli

My Lord, expand for me my breast [with assurance] and ease for me my task and untie the knot from my tongue that they may understand my speech.

Source: Surah Taha, 20:25-28

Story of Wisdom:

قَالَتْ نَمْلَةٌ يَا أَيُّهَا النَّمْلُ ادْخُلُوا مَسَاكِنَكُمْ لَا
يَحْطِمَنَّكُمْ سُلَيْمَانُ وَجُنُودُهُ وَهُمْ لَا يَشْعُرُونَ

Qalat namlatun ya ayyuha an-namlu adkhulu masakinakum la yahtimannakum Sulaimanu wa junooduhu wahum la yash'uroon

A single ant said, 'O ants, enter your dwellings! So, Solomon and his troops do not crush you unknowingly.'

Source: Qur'an, Surah An-Naml (27:18)

Dua for Strength and Vitality

اللّٰهُمَّ إِنِّي أَسْأَلُكَ العَفْوَ والعافِيةَ في الدنيا والآخِرةِ، اللّٰهُمَّ إِنِّي
أَسْأَلُكَ العَفْوَ والعافِيةَ في ديني ودنيايَ وأهلِي ومالِي، اللّٰهُمَّ استُر
عَوْراتِي وآمِنْ رَوعاتِي، اللّٰهُمَّ احفظْنِي مِن بينِ يدَيَّ ومِن خلفِي وعن
يمِينِي وعن شِمالِي، ومِن فوقِي وأعوذُ بِكَ أنْ أغتالَ مِن تحتِي

Allahumma inni as'aluka al-'afwa wal-'afiyata fid-dunya wal-akhirah.
Allahumma inni as'aluka al-'afwa wal-'afiyata fi dini wa dunyaya wa ahli wa
mali. Allahumma astur 'awrati wa amin raw'ati, Allahumma ihfadni min bayni
yadayya wa min khalfi wa 'an yamini wa 'an shimali, wa min fawqi, wa a'udhu
bika an ughtala min tahti.

Oh Allah, I ask you for pardon and well-being in this world and the next. Oh
Allah, I ask you for pardon and well-being in my religion, my worldly affairs,
my family and wealth. Oh Allah, conceal my faults, calm my fears, and protect
me from before me and behind me, from my right and my left, and from above
me, and I seek refuge in You from being taken unaware from beneath me.

Source: Sunan Abu Dawood, Hadith 5074

Story of Wisdom:

قال رسول الله صلى الله عليه وسلم: من قال حين يصبح
وحين يمسي: رضيت بالله ربا، وبالإسلام دينا، وبمحمد
نبيا، كان حقا على الله أن يرضيه يوم القيامة

Qala rasul Allahi salla Allah 'alayhi wa sallam: "man qala hina yusbihu wa
hina yumsi: raditu billahi rabban, wa bil-islami dinan, wa bi Muhammadin
nabiyyan, kana haqqan 'ala Allahi any yardiyah yawma al-qiyaamah"

The Prophet Muhammad (peace be upon him) said, "Whoever says when he
rises in the morning and when he retires in the evening: 'I am pleased with
Allah as my Lord, with Islam as my religion, and with Muhammad as my
Prophet,' it is a right upon Allah to please him on the Day of Judgment."

Source: Sunan Ibn Majah, Hadith 3800

Dua for a Healthy Life

اللَّهُمَّ أَعِنِّي عَلَى ذِكْرِكَ وَشُكْرِكَ وَحُسْنِ عِبَادَتِكَ

Allahumma a'inni 'ala dhikrika wa shukrika wa husni 'ibadatik.

O Allah, assist me in remembering You, in thanking You, and in worshipping You in the best of manners.

Source: Abu Dawood 1522.

Story of Wisdom:

عَنْ أَبِي هُرَيْرَةَ، قَالَ قَالَ رَسُولُ اللَّهِ صَلَّى اللهُ عَلَيْهِ وسلّم ,, أَيُّمَا رَجُلٍ سَارَ فِي طَرِيقٍ فَوَجَدَ غُصْنَ شَوْكٍ فَنَحَّاهُ عَنْهُ فَشَكَرَهُ اللَّهُ لَهُ فَغَفَرَ لَهُ "،

An abi hurayra, qala qala rasulullahi salla allahu alayhi wa sallam "ayyuma rajulin sara fi tariqin fawajada ghusna shawkin fanaza'ahu fashakarahu allahu lahu faghafara lahu."

Narrated by Abu Huraira: The Prophet said, "A man while walking along the path found a thorny branch of a tree on it. He removed it and Allah thanked him for that deed and forgave him."

Source: Sahih al-Bukhari 6525.

Dua for Protection from Diseases

بِسْمِ اللهِ الَّذِي لَا يَضُرُّ مَعَ اسْمِهِ شَيْءٌ فِي الْأَرْضِ وَلَا فِي السَّمَاءِ وَهُوَ السَّمِيعُ الْعَلِيمُ

Bismillahil-ladhee la yadurru ma'as-mihi shai'un fil-ardi wala fis-sama'i wahuwas-samee'ul-'aleem

In the name of Allah, with whose name nothing can cause harm on earth nor in the heavens, and He is the All-Hearing, All-Knowing.

Source: Abu Dawood 5088, At-Tirmidhi 3388.

Story of Wisdom:

قَالَ رَسُولُ اللَّهِ صَلَّى اللهُ عَلَيهِ وسَلَّمَ مَا أَصَابَ أَحَدًا قَطُّ هَمُّ الوَ
حَزَنٌ فَقَالَ اللَّهُمَّ إِنِّي عَبْدُكَ ابْنُ عَبْدِكَ ابْنُ أَمَتِكَ نَاصِيَتِي بِيَدِكَ
مَاضٍ فِيَّ حُكْمُكَ عَدْلٌ فِيَّ قَضَاؤُكَ أَسْأَلُكَ بِكُلِّ اسْمٍ هُوَ لَكَ سَمَّيْتَ بِهِ
نَفْسَكَ أَوْ أَنْزَلْتَهُ فِي كِتَابِكَ أَوْ عَلَّمْتَهُ أَحَدًا مِنْ خَلْقِكَ أَوِ اسْتَأْثَرْتَ
بِهِ فِي عِلْمِ الغَيْبِ عِنْدَكَ أَنْ تَجْعَلَ القُرْآنَ رَبِيعَ قَلْبِي وَنُورَ صَدْرِي
وَجَلَاءَ حُزْنِي وَذَهَابَ هَمِّيَ إِلَّا أَذْهَبَ اللَّهُ هَمَّهُ وَحَزَنَهُ وَأَبْدَلَهُ مَكَانَهُ فَرَجًا

Qala rasoolullahi sallallahu 'alayhi wasallam "ma asaba ahadan qattu hamun
wala hazanun faqala allahumma inni 'abduka ibnu 'abdika ibnu amatika
nasiyati biyadika madhin fiya hukmuka 'adlun fiya qada'uka as'aluka bikulli
ismin huwa laka sammayta bihi nafsaka aw anzaltahu fi kitabika aw
'allamtahu ahadan min khalqika awi ista'tharta bihi fi 'ilmil ghaybi 'indaka an
taj'ala alqur'ana rabia'a qalbi wa noora sadri wajala'a huzni wadhahaba hammi"
illa adhhaba allahu hammahu wazanahu wa abdalahau makanahu farajan

The Messenger of Allah (peace and blessings be upon him) said, "If anyone is
stricken with anxiety or sorrow and says: 'O Allah, I am Your servant, son of
Your male servant, son of Your female servant. My forelock is in Your hand,
Your command over me is forever executed and Your decree over me is just.
I ask You by every name belonging to You which You named Yourself with,
or revealed in Your Book, or You taught to any of Your creation, or You have
preserved in the knowledge of the unseen with You, that You make the Qur'an
the life of my heart and the light of my chest, and a departure for my sorrow
and a release for my anxiety,' Allah will remove his anxiety and sorrow and
replace it with joy."

Source: Al-Albani in Sahih At-Tirmidhi, Hadith: 2080.

Dua for Patience in Illness

إِنِّي مَسَّنِيَ الضُّرُّ وَأَنتَ أَرْحَمُ الرَّاحِمِينَ

Inni massaniya ad-durru wa anta arhamu ar-rahimin

Indeed, adversity has touched me, and You are the Most Merciful of the
merciful.

Source: Surah Al-Anbiya, 21:83

Story of Wisdom:

كَانَ الَّذِينَ مِن قَبْلِكُمُ يُؤَدُّونَ فِي الدُّخُودِ فَيُضَعُ فُونٌ فِيهَا وَيُشَرِّرُونَ
الْمِنَاشِيرَ عَلَى رُؤُوسِهِمْ وَيُمْشَطُونَ بِالْمَشَارِ وَمَا يَصُدُّهُمْ ذَلِكَ عَن دِينِهِمْ

Kaana alladheena min qablakum yuw'adoona al-luhud fa yudha'afuuna fiha
wa yusharrawna al-minaashir 'ala ruoosihim wa yumshatuuna bil-mishaari wa
ma yasudduhum dhalika 'an deenihim.

Those before you were literally taken to pits, then a saw was put over their
heads and they were sawn in half, and were scraped with iron combs off their
flesh and bones. Yet all this did not make them give up their faith.

Source: Sahih Bukhari 3612

Dua for Well-being of Children

رَبِّ اجْعَلْنِي مُقِيمَ الصَّلَاةِ وَمِن ذُرِّيَّتِي ۚ رَبَّنَا وَتَقَبَّلْ دُعَاءِ

Rabbi-ij'alni muqeemas salati, wa min dhurriyati, Rabbana wa taqabbal du'a

O my Lord! Make me one who performs As-Salat (the prayers), and (also)
from my offspring, our Lord! And accept my invocation.

Source: The Holy Qur'an, Surah Ibrahim (14:40)

Story of Wisdom:

إِذْ قَالَ لُقْمَانُ لِابْنِهِ وَهُوَ يَعِظُهُ يَا بُنَيَّ لَا تُشْرِكْ
بِاللَّهِ ۖ إِنَّ الشِّرْكَ لَظُلْمٌ عَظِيمٌ

Ith qala luqmanu li-ibnihi wa huwa ya'izuhu ya bunayya la tushrik billahi inna
ash-shirka la zulmun 'azim

When Luqman said to his son, as he advised him, "O my son, do not associate
anything with Allah. Indeed, association (with him) is a great injustice."

Source: The Holy Qur'an, Surah Luqman (31:13)

Dua for Healthy Eating Habits

اللّٰهُمَّ أَطْعِمْنِي حَلَالَ الطَّيِّبًا، وَاصْرِفْ عَنِّي حَرَامَهُ وَبِئْسَ الْحَلَفُ

Allahumma at'imnee halalan tayyiban, wasrif 'annee haramahu wa bi'sal halaf

Oh Allah, provide me with lawful (Halal) and good sustenance, and keep me away from the prohibited (Haram) and bad ones.

Source: Musnad Ahmad 17165

Story of Wisdom:

قَالَ يَا قَوْمِ اعْمَلُوا عَلَىٰ مَكَانَتِكُمْ إِنِّي عَامِلٌ سَوْفَ تَعْلَمُونَ مَنْ يَأْتِيهِ عَذَابٌ يُخْزِيهِ وَمَنْ هُوَ كَاذِبٌ وَارْتَقِبُوا إِنِّي مَعَكُمْ رَقِيبٌ

Qala ya qawmi'maloo 'ala makanatikum inni 'aamilun. Sawfa ta'lamoon man yateehi 'adhabun yukhzeehi wa man huwa kadhibun. Wa'rtqiboo inni ma'akum raqeeb.

He said, "Oh my people, you do your work in your position, and indeed, I am working. Soon you will know who will come upon him a punishment that will disgrace him and who is a liar. So watch; indeed, I am with you a watcher."

Source: Surah Hud (11:93)

Dua for Sound Sleep

بِاسْمِكَ رَبِّي وَضَعْتُ جَنْبِي، وَبِكَ أَرْفَعُهُ، فَإِنْ أَمْسَكْتَ نَفْسِي فَارْحَمْهَا، وَإِنْ أَرْسَلْتَهَا فَاحْفَظْهَا، بِمَا تَحْفَظُ بِهِ عِبَادَكَ الصَّالِحِينَ.

Bismika rabbi wada'tu janbi, wa bika arfa'uhu, fa in amsakta nafsi farhamha, wa in arsaltaha fahfazha, bima tahfazu bihi ibadakas saliheen.

In Your name, my Lord, I lie down, and in Your name I rise. If You hold my soul, be merciful to it, and if You release it, guard it as You guard your righteous servants.

Source: Sunan Abi Dawood 5045

Story of Wisdom:

عن عائشة رضي الله عنها قالت: قال رسول الله صلى الله
عليه وسلم: يا عائشة أرأيت لو كنت قبل أن يهديك الله
كيف كنت؟ قالت: الله ورسوله أعلم قال: يا عائشة! إن الله
تعالى يذهب بالليل ويأتي بالنهار، ويذهب بالنهار ويأتي
بالليل، وإن الشمس والقمر لا ينكسفان لموت أحد ولكنهما
آيتان من آيات الله، فإذا رأيتموهما فقوموا إلى الصلاة

عن عائشة رضي الله عنها قالت: قال رسول الله صلى الله
عليه وسلم: يا عائشة أرأيت لو كنت قبل أن يهديك الله
كيف كنت؟ قالت: الله ورسوله أعلم قال: يا عائشة! إن الله
تعالى يذهب بالليل ويأتي بالنهار، ويذهب بالنهار ويأتي
بالليل، وإن الشمس والقمر لا ينكسفان لموت أحد ولكنهما
آيتان من آيات الله، فإذا رأيتموهما فقوموا إلى الصلاة.

'An 'A'ishata radi Allahu 'anha qalat: qala rasul Allahi salla Allah 'alayh wa sallam: ya 'A'isha ara'ayt law kunt qabl an yahdiyak Allah kayf kunt? Qalat: Allah wa rasuluhu a'lam. Qala: ya 'A'isha! In Allah ta'ala yadhhab bil-layl wa yatee bin-nahar, wa yadhhab bin-nahar wa yatee bil-layl, wa in ash-shams wa al-qamar la yankasifan limawt ahad walakin huma ayatan min ayat Allah, fa idha ra'aytumuha faqumoo ila as-salah.

On the authority of Aisha, may Allah be pleased with her, she said: The Messenger of Allah, peace and blessings be upon him, said: "O Aisha, do you see if you were before Allah guided you, how you were?" She said: "Allah and His Messenger know best." He said: "O Aisha! Indeed, the Most High makes the night pass and brings the day, and makes the day pass and brings the night, and indeed the sun and moon do not eclipse for the death of anyone, but they are signs among the signs of Allah, so when you see them, rise for prayer."

Source: Sahih al-Bukhari 1064

Dua for Ease and Comfort

اَللّٰهُمَّ لَا سَهْلَ إِلَّا مَا جَعَلْتَهُ سَهْلًا وَ أَنْتَ تَجْعَلُ الْحَزْنَ إِذَا شِئْتَ سَهْلًا

Allahumma la sahla illa ma ja'altahu sahlan, wa 'anta taj'alul hazna idha shi'ta sahlan.

Oh Allah, there is no ease except in that which You have made easy, and You make the difficulty, if You wish, easy.

Source: Sunan Ibn Majah 3435

Story of Wisdom:

قَالَ رَسُولُ اللّٰهِ صَلَّى اللّٰهُ عَلَيْهِ وسلَّم: لَا يَمُنَّنَّ أَحَدُكُمْ نَفْسَهُ، وَلَكِنْ لِيَقُلِ: اَللّٰهُمَّ أَحْيِنِي مَا كَانَتِ الْحَيَاةُ خَيْرًا لِي، وَتَوَفَّنِي إِذَا كَانَتِ الْوَفَاةُ خَيْرًا لِي

Qala rasool Allahi salla Allah alayhi wa sallam: "La yamunnanna ahadukum nafsahu, walakin liyaquli: Allahumma ahyini ma kanatil hayatu khairan li, wa tawaffani idha kanatil wafatu khairan li."

The Messenger of Allah, peace and blessings be upon him, said: "None of you should wish for death because of a calamity befalling him; but if he has to wish for death, he should say: 'O Allah! Keep me alive as long as life is better for me, and let me die if death is better for me.'"

Source: Sahih al-Bukhari 5671

Dua for Spiritual Cleanliness

اَللّٰهُمَّ إِنِّي أَعُوذُ بِكَ مِنَ الْبَرَصِ، وَالْجُنُونِ، وَالْجُذَامِ، وَمِنْ سَيِّئِ الْأَسْقَامِ

Allahumma inni a'udhu bika min al-barasi, wal-junooni, wal-judhaami, wa min sayyi'il-asqaami

O Allah, I take refuge in You from leprosy, insanity, leucoderma, and evil diseases.

Source: Sahih al-Bukhari 5755

Story of Wisdom:

قَالَ رَسُولُ اللَّهِ صَلَّى اللهُ عَلِيهِ وسلم: "لَا يُؤْمِنُ
أَحَدُكُمْ حَتَّى يُحِبَّ لِأَخِيهِ مَا يُحِبُّ لِنَفْسِهِ

Qala rasoolullahi salla Allah alayhi wasallam: "laa yu'minu ahadukum hattaa yuhibba li-akheehi ma yuhibbu li-nafsihi."

The Prophet Muhammad (peace be upon him) said: "None of you truly believes until he loves for his brother what he loves for himself."

Source: Sahih al-Bukhari 13

Chapter 5:
Self-Improvement Journey: Duas
for Personal Development

Dua for Seeking Forgiveness

اللّهُمَّ أنتَ رَبّي لا إلَه إلا أنتَ خَلَقْتَني وأنا عبدُكَ وأنا على عَهدِكَ
ووَعدِكَ ما استطعتُ أعوذُ بكَ مِن شرِّ ما صنعتُ أبوءُ لكَ بنِعمتِكَ
علَيَّ وأبوءُ بذنبي فاغفِرْ لي فإنَّه لا يغفِرُ الذنوبَ إلا أنتَ

Allahumma anta rabbi, la ilaha illa anta, khalaqtani wa ana abduka, wa ana 'ala ahdika wa wa'dika ma astata'tu. A'udhu bika min sharri ma sana'tu, abu'u laka bi ni'matika 'alayya, wa abu'u bi dhanbi, faghfir li, fa innahu la yaghfirudh-dhunuba illa anta.

O Allah, You are my Lord, there is no deity but You. You have created me, and I am Your servant, and I am on Your covenant and promise as much as I can. I seek refuge with You from the evil of what I have done, I acknowledge Your favor upon me, and I acknowledge my sin, so forgive me, for no one forgives sins but You.

Source: Sahih al-Bukhari 6306

Story of Wisdom:

قال رسولُ اللهِ صلى اللهُ عليهِ وسلمَ: من قال حينَ
يصبحُ وحينَ يمسي: رضيتُ باللهِ ربًّا، وبالإسلامِ
ديِنًا، وبمحمدٍ نبيًّا، فأنا الزعيمُ لأدخِلنَّهُ اللهُ الجنةَ

Qala rasool Allahi salla Allahi 'alayhi wa sallama: man qala hiyn yusbihu wa hiyn yamsi: radiytu billahi rabban, wa bil-islami deenan, wa biMuhammadin nabiyyan, fa ana al-za'eem la'udkhalannahu Allahu al-jannah.

The Prophet Muhammad, peace be upon him, said: Whoever says when he rises in the morning and when the evening comes: "I am pleased with Allah as my Lord, Islam as my religion, and Muhammad as my Prophet", then I guarantee that Allah will certainly admit him to Paradise.

Source: Sunan Ibn Majah 3800

Dua for Guidance and Knowledge

اللَّهُمَّ رَبَّ جِبْرِيلَ وَمِيكَائِيلَ وَإِسْرَافِيلَ، فَاطِرَ السَّمَاوَاتِ
وَالْأَرْضِ، عَالِمَ الْغَيْبِ وَالشَّهَادَةِ، أَنْتَ تَحْكُمُ بَيْنَ عِبَادِكَ
فِيمَا كَانُوا فِيهِ يَخْتَلِفُونَ. اهْدِنِي لِمَا اخْتُلِفَ فِيهِ مِنَ الْحَقِّ
بِإِذْنِكَ، إِنَّكَ تَهْدِي مَنْ تَشَاءُ إِلَى الصِّرَاطِ الْمُسْتَقِيمِ

Allahumma rabbu Jibril wa Mika'il wa Israfil, fatir al-samawati wal-ard,
'alim al-ghaib wa al-shahadah, anta tahkumu bayna 'ibadik fi ma kanu fihi
yakhtalifun. Ihdini lima ikhtulifa fihi min al-haq bi idhnik, innaka tahdi man
tasha ila sirat mustaqim.

Oh Allah, Lord of Gabriel, Michael, and Raphael, creator of the heavens
and the earth, knower of the unseen and the witness, you decide among your
servants in what they differ. Guide me to the truth in what they differ about,
by your permission, for you guide whom you will to a straight path.

Source: Tirmidhi 3241

Story of Wisdom:

إِذْ قَالَ مُوسَىٰ لِفَتَاهُ لَا أَبْرَحُ حَتَّىٰ أَبْلُغَ مَجْمَعَ الْبَحْرَيْنِ أَوْ أَمْضِيَ حُقُبًا

Ith qala Musa lifatahu la abrahu hatta ablugha majma'al-bahrayni aw amdiya
huquba.

When Moses said to his attendant, "I will not cease traveling until I reach the
junction of the two seas or continue for a long period."

Source: Qur'an 18:60

Dua for Overcoming Laziness

اللَّهُمَّ إِنِّي أَعُوذُ بِكَ مِنَ الْعَجْزِ وَالْكَسَلِ

Allahumma inni a'udhu bika minal-'ajzi wal-kasal

O Allah, I seek refuge with You from incapacity and laziness.

Story of Wisdom:

قال رسول الله: ,,اليد العليا خير من اليد السفلى،
وابدأ بمن تعول، وخير الصدقة عن ظهر غنى، ومن
يستعفف يعفه الله، ومن يستغن يغنه الله"

Qala rasulullah: "Al-yadu al-'ulya khayrun min al-yadis-sufli, wa-bda' biman ta'ul, wa khayru sadaqatin 'an zuhri ghina, wa man yasta'iff yu'iffuhu allah, wa man yastaghni yughnih Allah"

The Messenger of Allah said: "The upper hand is better than the lower hand (he who gives is better than him who takes). Start giving first to your dependents. The best charity is that which is given out of surplus wealth. And he who asks Allah to help him abstain from the unlawful and the forbidden, Allah will fulfill his wish; and he who seeks self-sufficiency will be made self-sufficient by Allah."

Source: Sahih al-Bukhari 1427

Dua for Strength and Courage

اللّهمّ ال سهل ال إلا ما جعلته سهلا وأنت تجعل الحزن إذا شئت سهلا

Allahumma la sahla illa ma ja'altahu sahla, wa 'anta taj'alul hazna idha shi'ta sahla

Oh Allah, there is no ease except in that which You have made easy. If You wish, You can make the difficult easy.

Source: Sahih Ibn Hibban

Story of Wisdom:

قال رسول الله صلّى الله عليه وسلّم: ,,إذا
أحسن العبد خلقه أحسن الله صورته"

Qala rasool Allahi salla Allah alayhi wa sallam: "Idha ahsana a'abdu khuluqahu, ahsana Allahu suratahu".

The Messenger of Allah, peace and blessings upon him, said: "When a servant improves his character, Allah improves his appearance."

Source: Musnad Ahmad.

Dua for Success in Exams and Interviews

اللّهمّ ال سهل ال ام اإلذ جعلته سهال أو انت تجعل الحزن اذإ شئت سهال

Allahumma la sahla illa ma ja'altahu sahla, wa 'anta taj'alul hazna idha shi'ta sahla.

Oh Allah, no task is easy except what You render easy, and You can render sadness into ease should You wish.

Source: Ibn Hibban in his Sahih, 2422.

Story of Wisdom:

قال رجل من األنصار صلى هللا عليه وسلم: اي رسول هللا، فقال النبيّي صلى هللا عليه ال تدع لنا ممّا ينتفع الناس به. اللّهمّ: وسلم أغنِنا بحالالك عن حرامكَ، وبفضلكَ عمّن سواكَ

Qala rajulun min al-Ansar li al-Nabiyyi salla Allah 'alayhi wa sallam: Ya Rasul Allah, la tad'u lana mimma yuntafa'u al-nasu bih. Faqala al-Nabiyyu salla Allah 'alayhi wa sallam: Allahumma aghnina bihalalika 'an haramika, wabifadlika 'amman siwaka.

A man from the Ansar said to Prophet Muhammad, peace be upon him: Oh Messenger of Allah, do not pray for us from what people benefit. The Prophet, peace be upon him, responded: Oh Allah, enrich us with Your halal (permissible) over Your haram (prohibited), and by Your grace over anyone else.

Source: Sunan At-Tirmidhi, 3563.

Dua for Rectification of Character

Dua for Wealth and Sustenance

رَبَّنَا آتِنا مِن لَدُنكَ رِزقًا حَسَنًا وَقِنا عَذابَ النَّارِ

Rabbana atina min ladunka rizqan hasanan wa qina 'adhaban-nar

Our Lord, grant us from Yourself good provision and protect us from the punishment of the Fire.

Source: Surah Al-Baqarah, 2:201

Story of Wisdom:

قَالَ النَّبِيُّ صَلَّى اللهُ عَلَيْهِ وسلَّمَ، إِنَّ ما نَقَصَتْ صَدَقَةٌ مِّنْ مَالٍ وَمَا
زَادَ اللهُ عَبْدًا بِعَفْوِ الّا عِزًّا، وَمَا تَوَاضَعَ أَحَدٌ لِلَّهِ الّا رَفَعَهُ اللهُ

Qala al-nabiyyu, salla Allahu 'alayhi wa sallam, "ma naqasat sadaqatun min malin, wa ma zada Allahu 'abdan bi'afwin illa 'izzan, wa ma tawada'a ahadun lillahi illa rafa'ahu Allah."

The Prophet, peace be upon him, said, "Charity does not decrease wealth, no one forgives another except that Allah increases his honor, and no one humbles himself for the sake of Allah except that Allah raises his status."

Source: Sahih Muslim 2588.

Dua for Repentance and Turning to Allah

اللَّهُمَّ أَنْتَ رَبِّي لَا إِلَهَ إِلَّا أَنْتَ خَلَقْتَنِي وَأَنَا عَبْدُكَ وَأَنَا عَلَى عَهْدِكَ
وَوَعْدِكَ مَا اسْتَطَعْتُ أَعُوذُ بِكَ مِنْ شَرِّ مَا صَنَعْتُ أَبُوءُ لَكَ بِنِعْمَتِكَ
عَلَيَّ وَأَبُوءُ بِذَنْبِي فَاغْفِرْ لِي فَإِنَّهُ لَا يَغْفِرُ الذُّنُوبَ إِلَّا أَنْتَ

Allahumma anta rabbi la ilaha illa anta, khalaqtani wa ana 'abduka, wa ana 'ala 'ahdika wa wa'dika mastata'tu, a'udhu bika min sharri ma sana'tu, abu'u laka bini'matika 'alayya, wa abu'u bidhanbi faghfir li fa'innahu la yaghfirudh-dhunuba illa anta

O Allah! You are my Lord! None has the right to be worshipped but You. You created me and I am Your slave, and I am faithful to my covenant and my promise as much as I can. I seek refuge with You from all the evil I have done. I acknowledge before You all the blessings You have bestowed upon me, and I confess to You all my sins. So, I entreat You to forgive my sins, for nobody can forgive sins except You.

Source: Sahih al-Bukhari 6306

Story of Wisdom:

قَالَ رَجُلٌ مِّنَ الْقَوْمِ يَا رَسُولَ اللهِ إِنَّ شَرَائِعَ الإِسْلامِ قَدْ كَثُرَتْ عَلَيَّ
فَأَخْبِرْنِي بِشَيْءٍ أَتَشَبَّثُ بِهِ قَالَ لَا يَزَالُ لِسَانُكَ رَطْبًا مِّنْ ذِكْرِ اللهِ

Qala rajulun mina al-qawmi ya rasula allah, inna shara-i'a al-islam qad kathurat 'alayya fa akhbirni bi shay'in atashabbathu bihi. Qala la yazalu lisanuka ratban min dhikri allah

A man said to the Prophet, 'The laws of Islam are too heavy for me, so tell me something that I can easily follow,' the Prophet replied, 'Let your tongue always be moist with the remembrance of Allah.'

Source: Jami` at-Tirmidhi 3375

Dua for Protection from Misguidance

اللّهّمّ إنّي أعوذ بك من الضّلال والبّلال، ومن
الجهل والزلل، ومن تيّارا الشقاق

Allahumma inni a'udhu bika minad-dalali wal-balal, wa min al-jahl wa-z-zillal, wa min tiyare ash-shiqaq.

Oh Allah, I seek refuge with You from straying and being led astray, from ignorance and from missteps, and from the divisive discord.

Source: Sahih al-Tirmidhi 3600

Story of Wisdom:

قَالَ رَسُولُ اللّهِ صَلَّى اللّهُ عَلَيْهِ وَسَلَّمَ: إِنَّ اللّهَ يُحِبُّ
الْمُؤْمِنَ الْقَوِيَّ أَكْثَرَ مِنَ الْمُؤْمِنِ الضَّعِيفِ وَفِي كُلِّ خَيْرٍ،
احْرِصْ عَلَى مَا يَنْفَعُكَ وَاسْتَعِنْ بِاللّهِ وَلَا تَعْجَزْ.

Qala rasoolu Allahi salla Allahu alayhi wa sallam: Inna Allaha yuhibbu al-mu'min al-qawi akthara min al-mu'min ad-daeef wa fi kullin khayr, ihriṣ 'ala ma yanfa'uk wa ista'in billahi wa la ta'jaz.

The Messenger of Allah, peace be upon him, said: "Indeed, Allah loves the strong believer more than the weak believer, but there is good in everyone. Be eager for what benefits you, seek help from Allah, and do not lose courage."

Source: Sahih Muslim 2664.

Dua for Patience and Perseverance

انَمَادقْأَ تْـبِّـثَوَ ارًبْـصَ انَيْلَعَ غْرِفْأَ انَبَّرَ

نَيِرِفـاكَلْا مِوْقَلْا ىلَعَ انَرْصُنْاوَ

Rabbana afrigh 'alayna sabran wa thabbit aqdamana wa ansurna 'ala al-qawmi al-kafireen

Our Lord, pour upon us patience, firm our steps, and help us against the disbelieving people

Source: Surah Al-Baqarah, 2:250

Story of Wisdom:

جرفـلا حاتـفم ربـصصلا :ملّسو هيلع هللا ىلّص يّبنّلا لاق

Qala an-nabiyy salla Allahu 'alayhi wa sallam: as-sabr miftah al-faraj

The Prophet, peace be upon him, said: "Patience is the key to relief."

Source: Sunan Ibn Majah 4032

Dua for Removal of Worries and Depression

ضامٍ ،كَدِيَبِ يتِيصِان ،كِتِمَأُ نْبا ،كَدِبْعَ نْبا ،كَدُبْعَ ينِّإ مّهُللَّا
يفِ ّرْحُ كُمْكَ ،كَؤُاضَقَ يَّفِ لْدْعَ ،كُمْكُحَ ّيَفِ نْسَمِّتَ
بهَ نْفَسَكَ وْأَ ،كَنْزَلْتُهُ يفِ كِباتَك وْأَ كَعَمْتَلَّمْتُهُ ادَحْأَ نْم كَقْلْخَ ،وْأَ
اسَأتْثَرتَ هبِ يفِ مْلْعِ بْيَغْلْا كَنْدْعَ ،نْأَ تَجْعَلَ لْقُرْآنَ لْعَظيمَ
ربيعَ قَلْبِي ،وَنُورَ صَدْري ،وَجِلاءَ خُزْنِي ،وَذَهابَ هَمِّي

Allahumma inni 'abduka, ibnu 'abdika, ibnu amatika, nasiyati biyadika, madin fiyya hukmuka, 'adlun fiyya qada'uka, as'aluka biko lli ismin huwa laka, sammayta bihi nafsaka, aw anzaltahu fi kitabika, aw 'allamtahu ahadan min khalqika, aw ista'tharta bihi fi 'ilm al-ghayb 'indaka, an taj'al al-Qur'ana al-'azima rabee'a qalbi, wa nur sadri, wa jila'a huzni, wa dhahaba hammi

O Allah, I am Your servant, son of Your servant, son of Your maidservant; my forelock is in Your hand, Your command over me is forever executed and Your decree over me is just. I ask You by every name belonging to You which You named Yourself with, or revealed in Your Book, or You taught to any of Your creation, or You have preserved in the knowledge of the unseen with You, that You make the Quran the life of my heart and the light of my chest, and a departure for my sorrow and a release for my anxiety

Story of Wisdom:

قَالَ اللّٰهُ كَتَبَ عَلَى نَفْسِهِ الرَّحْمَةَ لَيَجْمَعَنَّكُمْ إِلَى يَوْمِ الْقِيَامَةِ
لَا رَيْبَ فِيهِ الَّذِينَ خَسِرُوا أَنْفُسَهُمْ فَهُمُ الْمُؤْمِنُونَ

Qala Allahu kataba 'ala nafsihi al-rahmah layajma'annakum ila yawm al-qiyamah la rayba feehi allatheena khasiroo anfusahum fahum la yu'minoon

Allah has prescribed mercy upon Himself, He will surely gather you on the Day of Resurrection, there is no doubt about it. Those who have ruined themselves will not believe.

Source: Qur'an 6:12

Dua for Clarity and Decision Making

اللّٰهُمَّ اهْدِنِي وَسَدِّدْنِي

Allahumma ihdini wasaddidni

Oh Allah, guide me and set me straight.

Source: Sahih Muslim 2705

Story of Wisdom:

حَدَّثَنَا ابْنُ أَبِي عُمَرَ، وَأَصْحَابُ الشَّأْنِ، وَهُمْ أَرْبَعَةٌ جَمِيعًا عَنْ سُفْيَانَ،
عَنْ عَمْرِو بْنِ دِينَارٍ، عَنْ جَابِرِ بْنِ عَبْدِ اللّٰهِ، أَنَّ رَجُلًا غَدَا إِلَى النَّبِيِّ
صَلَّى اللّٰهُ عَلَيْهِ وسلم فَقَالَ يَا رَسُولَ اللّٰهِ، أَلَمْ أَرَكَ تَعُودُ إِلَى اللّٰهِ
وَتَسْتَهْدِيهِ قَبْلَ أَنْ تَعْتَدِيَ قَالَ: نَعَمْ، إِنِّي أَعُودُ إِلَى اللّٰهِ وَأَسْتَهْدِيهِ
قَبْلَ أَنْ أَعْتَدِيَ، اللّٰهُمَّ اهْدِنِي فِيمَنْ هَدَيْتَ، وَعَافِنِي فِيمَنْ عَافَيْتَ

Hadathana ibnu abi 'amr wa as'habu alsha'n wa hum 'arba'tun jamian 'an sufyan, 'an 'amr bin dīnar, 'an jabir bin 'abd allah, anna rajulan, ghada ila alnnabiyyi salla allahu alaihi wasallam faqala ya rasul allah, alam arak ta'ud ila allah wa tastahdih qabl an ta'tadi. Qala: na'am, inni a'ud ila allah wa astahdih qabl an a'tadi, allahumma ihdini fiman hadayt, wa 'afini fiman 'afayt.

It was narrated to us by Ibn Abi Amro and the companions of the matter, all four of them, from Sufyan, from Amro bin Dinar, from Jabir bin Abdullah, that a man came to the Prophet (peace be upon him) and said, "O Messenger of Allah, have I not seen you return to Allah and seek His guidance before you transgress." He said, "Yes, indeed, I return to Allah and seek His guidance before I transgress. Oh Allah, guide me among those whom You have guided, and pardon me among those whom You have pardoned."

Source: Sunan Al-Nasa'i 5489

Chapter 6:
Community Well-being: Duas for Social Responsibility and Engagement

Dua for Unity Among Muslims

اللّٰهُمَّ أَلِّفْ بَيْنَ قُلُوبِنَا، وَأَصْلِحْ ذَاتَ بَيْنِنَا، وَاهْدِنَا السُّبُلَ السَّلَامِ، وَنَجِّنَا مِنَ الظُّلُمَاتِ إِلَى النُّورِ، وَجَنِّبْنَا الْفَوَاحِشَ مَا ظَهَرَ مِنْهَا وَمَا بَطَنَ

Allahumma alif bayna qulubina, wa aslih dhaata baynina, wahdina subul assalam, wa najjina mina azzulumati ila annur, wa jannibna al fawahisha ma dhahara minha wa ma batan.

O Allah, reconcile our hearts, rectify the relations between us, guide us on the path of peace, deliver us from darkness into light, and keep us away from all obscenities, both hidden and open.

Source: Sunan Abi Dawood

Story of Wisdom:

قَالَ رَسُولُ اللّٰهِ صَلَّى اللّٰهُ عَلَيْهِ وَسَلَّمَ: "لَا يُؤْمِنُ أَحَدُكُمْ حَتَّى يُحِبَّ لِأَخِيهِ مَا يُحِبُّ لِنَفْسِهِ"

Qaal rasool Allahi salla Allah alaihi wa sallam: "la yu'minu ahadukum hatta yuhibba li akhihi ma yuhibbu linafsihi"

The Prophet Muhammad peace be upon him said: "None of you will have faith till he loves for his brother what he loves for himself."

Source: Sahih al-Bukhari 13

Dua for the Well-being of the Ummah

اللّهَمّ اهدنا فيمن هديت، وعافنا فيمن عافيت، وتولّنا فيمن توليت،
وبارك لنا فيما أعطيت، وقنا واصرف عنّا شرّ ما قضيت، إنّك تقضي
ولا يقضى عليك، إنّه لا يذلّ من واليت، تباركت ربّنا وتعاليت

Allahumma ahdina feeman hadayt, wa 'afina feeman 'afayt, wa tawallana feeman tawallayt, wa barik lana feema 'a'tayt, wa qina wasrif 'anna sharra ma qadayt, innaka taqdi wa la yuqda 'alayk, innahu la yadhillu man walaayt, tabarakta rabbana wa ta'alayt.

Oh Allah, guide us among those whom You have guided, pardon us among those whom You have pardoned, befriend us among those whom You have befriended, bless us in whatever You grant us, and protect us and divert from us the evil which You have decreed. For You decree in truth, and none can decree over You. Truly, he whom You befriend is not disgraced. You are Blessed, our Lord, and Exalted.

Source: Sahih Muslim 2736a

Story of Wisdom:

قال النبيّ محمد صلّى الله عليه وسلّم: ,,ال تحاسدوا وال
تناجشوا وال تباغضوا وال تدابروا وال يبع بعضكم
على بيع بعض وكونوا عباد الله إخوانا''

Qala an-nabiyyu Muhammadun sallallahu 'alayhi wa sallam: "La tahasado wa la tanajasho wa la tabaghado wa la tadabaro wa la yabi' ba'dukum 'ala bayi' ba'din wa kunu ibad Allahi ikhwana"

Prophet Muhammad said: "Do not envy each other, do not inflate prices for each other, do not hate each other, do not turn away from each other, and do not undercut each other in trade, but rather be slaves of Allah and brothers amongst yourselves."

Source: Sahih Muslim 2564a

Dua for Leaders and Decision Makers

اللَّهُمَّ يَا مُقَلِّبَ الْقُلُوبِ ثَبِّتْ قَلْبِي عَلَى دِينِكَ

Allahumma Ya Muqallib al-Quloob Thabbit Qalbi 'Ala Deenik

O Allah, changer of hearts, make my heart firm upon Your religion.

Source: Sunan Tirmidhi 2140

Story of Wisdom:

قَالَ رَسُولُ اللهِ صَلَّى اللهُ عَلَيْهِ وسَلَّمَ إِنَّ الْمُؤْمِنَ الْقُوِيَّ خَيْرٌ وَأَحَبُّ إِلَى اللهِ مِنَ الْمُؤْمِنِ الضَّعِيفِ وَفِي كُلِّ خَيْرٌ احْرِصْ عَلَى مَا يَنْفَعُكَ واسْتَعِنْ باللهِ وَلَا تَعْجِزْ وَإِنْ أَصَابَكَ شَيْءٌ فَلَا تَقُلْ لَوْ أَنِّي فَعَلْتُ كَانَ كَذَا وَكَذَا وَلَكِنْ قُلْ قَدَرُ اللهِ وَمَا شَاءَ فَعَلَ فَإِنَّ لَوْ تَفْتَحُ عَمَلَ الشَّيْطَانِ

Qala rasool Allahi salla Allah alaihe wa sallam: al-mu'min al-qawiyyu khayrun wa ahabbu ila Allahi min al-mu'min al-da'ifi wa fi kullin khayrun. Ihris 'ala ma yanfa'uka, waistain billahi wala ta'jaz. Wa in asabaka shay'un falataqul law anni fa'altu kana katha wa katha. Walakin qul: qadar Allahi wama sha'a fa'ala. Fa'inna law taftahu 'amal al-Shaitan.

The Messenger of Allah (peace and blessings be upon him) said, "The strong believer is better and more beloved to Allah than the weak believer, but there is good in everyone. Strive for what benefits you, seek help from Allah, and do not be helpless. If something bothers you, do not say, 'If I had done such and such, then such and such would have happened.' But say: 'This is the decree of Allah and what He has willed, He has done.' For 'if' opens the door for the work of the devil."

Source: Sahih Muslim 2664.

Dua for the Oppressed and Suffering

اللَّهُمَّ إِنِّي أَسْأَلُكَ الْعَفْوَ وَالْعَافِيَةَ فِي الدُّنْيَا وَالْآخِرَةِ، اللَّهُمَّ إِنِّي أَسْأَلُكَ الْعَفْوَ وَالْعَافِيَةَ فِي دِينِي وَدُنْيَايَ وَأَهْلِي وَمَالِي، اللَّهُمَّ اسْتُرْ عَوْرَاتِي وَآمِنْ رَوْعَاتِي، اللَّهُمَّ احْفَظْنِي مِنْ بَيْنِ يَدَيَّ وَمِنْ خَلْفِي وَعَنْ يَمِينِي وَعَنْ شِمَالِي وَمِنْ فَوْقِي، وَأَعُوذُ بِعَظَمَتِكَ أَنْ أُغْتَالَ مِنْ تَحْتِي

Allahumma inni as'aluka al-'afwa wal-'afiyata fid-dunya wal-akhirah. Allahumma inni as'aluka al-'afwa wal-'afiyata fi dini wa dunyai wa ahli wa mali. Allahumma astur 'aurati wa aman raw'ati, Allahumma ihfazni min bayni yadayya wa min khalfi wa 'an yamini wa 'an shimali wa min fawqi, wa a'udhu bi'azamatika an ughtala min tahti.

Oh Allah, I ask You for pardon and wellbeing in this life and the next. Oh Allah, I ask You for pardon and wellbeing in my religious and worldly affairs, and in my family and property. Oh Allah, cover my faults, calm my fears, protect me from in front of me and behind me, to my right and my left and from above me, and I seek refuge in Your greatness from being killed from below me.

Source: Jami` at-Tirmidhi 3488.

Story of Wisdom:

قال النبيّ صلّى الله عليه وسلّم: "إنّ الله
يحبّ إذا عمل أحدكم عملًا أن يتقنه."

Qala an-nabi salla Allahu 'alayhi wa sallam: "Inna Allaha yuhibbu idha 'amila ahadukum 'amalan an yatqinahu."

The Prophet, peace be upon him, said, "Allah loves when one of you performs a deed, that he perfects it."

Source: Sahih al-Bukhari 6059.

Dua for Peace and Harmony in Society

رَبَّنَا آتِنَا فِي الدُّنْيَا حَسَنَةً وَفِي الآخِرَةِ حَسَنَةً وَقِنَا عَذَابَ النَّارِ

Allahumma Rabbanaa aatinaa fiddunyaa hasanah, wa fil-akhirati hasanah, wa qinaa adhaban-nar

O Allah, our Lord, give us good in this world and good in the Hereafter, and protect us from the punishment of the Fire.

Source: Surah Al-Baqarah, 2:201

Story of Wisdom:

قَالَ مُوسَىٰ لِقَوْمِهِ اسْتَعِينُوا بِاللَّهِ وَاصْبِرُوا ۖ إِنَّ الْأَرْضَ
لِلَّهِ يُورِثُهَا مَن يَشَاءُ مِنْ عِبَادِهِ ۖ وَالْعَاقِبَةُ لِلْمُتَّقِينَ

Qala Moosa liqawmihi ista'eenu billahi wasbiru, inna al-arda lillahi yurithuha man yasha'u min ibadihi, wal-aqibatu lilmuttaqin.

Moses said to his people, "Seek help through Allah and be patient. Indeed, the earth belongs to Allah. He gives it as inheritance to whom He wills of His servants. And the [best] outcome is for the righteous."

Source: Surah Al-A'raf, 7:128

Dua for the Eradication of Poverty

اللّٰهُمَّ اكفِني بِحلالِك عن حرامِك، وأغنِني بفضلِك عمّن سواك

Allahumma kafini bihalalika 'an haramika, wa aghnini bifadlika 'amman siwaka

Oh Allah, suffice me with Your lawful against Your forbidden, and make me independent of all those besides You.

Source: Sunan Abi Dawood 5082

Story of Wisdom:

قَالَ مُوسَىٰ لِقَوْمِهِ اسْتَعِينُوا بِاللَّهِ وَاصْبِرُوٓاۖ إِنَّ ٱلْأَرْضَ لِلَّهِ يُورِثُهَا مَن يَشَآءُ مِنْ عِبَادِهِۦۖ وَٱلْعَٰقِبَةُ لِلْمُتَّقِينَ

Qala Musa liqawmihi ista'eenu billahi wasbiroo. Inna al-arda lillahi yoorithuha man yasha'u min ibadihi. Wal aqibatu lilmuttaqeen

Moses said to his people: "Seek help in Allah and endure. Verily, the earth belongs to Allah. He gives it as a heritage to whom He wills of His slaves, and the successful outcome is for those who are God-fearing."

Source: Holy Qur'an 7:128

Dua for Sincerity in Helping Others

اللّٰهُمّ اكفِنِي بِحَلالِك عَنْ حَرَامِك أَوْ غْنِنِي بَفَضْلِكَ عَمَّ سِوَاكَ

Allahumma kfini bihalalika 'an haramika wa aghnini bifadlika 'amman siwaka

O Allah, suffice me with Your lawful against Your prohibited, and make me independent of all those besides You.

Source: Sahih al-Tirmidhi 3563

Story of Wisdom:

وَكَانَ رَجُلٌ مِنَ الْأَنْصَارِ يُدْعَى أَبُو بِنَادٍ، وَكَانَ يَتَصَدَّقُ بِجُودٍ
وَسَخَاءٍ. يَوْمًا، أَتَى رَسُولَ اللَّهِ صَلَّى اللَّهُ عَلَيْهِ وَسَلَّمَ بِعِنَاقٍ
كَبِيرٍ مِنَ الطَّعَامِ وَقَالَ: "يَا رَسُولَ اللَّهِ، إِنِّي قَدْ تَصَدَّقْتُ بِهَذَا عَلَى
فُقَرَاءِ الْمُسْلِمِينَ." فَقَالَ رَسُولُ اللَّهِ صَلَّى اللَّهُ عَلَيْهِ وَسَلَّمَ:
"بَارَكَ اللَّهُ فِيكَ وَفِي مَا عَطَاكَ. إِنَّكَ قَدْ كُنْتَ قُدْوَةً لِلْخَيْرِ."

Wa kana rajulun mina al-ansari yuda'u abu binadin, wa kana yatasaddaqu
bijoodin wasakha. Yawman, ataa rasool allah salla allahu alaihi wa salam
bi'inaqin kabirin mina altta'ami wa qala: "Ya rasool allah, inni qad tasaddaqtu
bihatha 'ala fuqarae almuslimeen." Faqala rasool allah salla allahu alaihi wa
salam: "Barak allah feek wa fee ma 'ataak. Innaka qad kunta qudwatan lilkhair."

There was a man from the Ansar called Abu Binad, who was known for his
generosity and benevolence. One day, he came to the Prophet Muhammad,
peace be upon him, with a large bundle of food and said: "O Messenger of
Allah, I have given this as charity to the poor Muslims." The Prophet, peace
be upon him, said: "May Allah bless you and what He has given you. You have
indeed been a role model for goodness."

Source: Sahih al-Bukhari 5868

Dua for Forgiveness for the Entire Ummah

اللَّهُمَّ اغْفِرْ لِي وَلِوَالِدَيَّ وَلِلْمُؤْمِنِينَ وَالْمُؤْمِنَاتِ
وَالْمُسْلِمِينَ وَالْمُسْلِمَاتِ الْأَحْيَاءِ مِنْهُمْ وَالْأَمْوَاتِ

Allahumma ighfir li, wa liwalidayya, wa lil mu'mineena wa'l mu'minaati, wa'l
muslimina wa'l muslimaati, al-ahyaai minhum wal-amwat.

Oh Allah, forgive me, my parents, and the believing men and women, the
Muslim men and women, those who are alive and those who have passed.

Source: Jami` at-Tirmidhi 1983

Story of Wisdom:

قَالَ رَسُولُ اللَّهِ صَلَّى اللَّهُ عَلَيْهِ وسَلَّمَ, إِلَا يُؤْمِنُ
أَحَدُكُمْ حَتَّى يُحِبَّ لِأَخِيهِ مَا يُحِبُّ لِنَفْسِهِ

Qala Rasul Allahi salla Allah 'alayh wa sallam "La yu'minu ahadukum hatta yuhibba li-akheehi ma yuhibbu li-nafsih."

The Messenger of Allah, peace and blessings be upon him, said: None of you truly believes until he loves for his brother what he loves for himself.

Source: Sahih al-Bukhari 13

Dua for Protection from Disunity and Conflict

اللَّهُمَّ أَلِّفْ بَيْنَ قُلُوبِنَا وَأَصْلِحْ ذَاتَ بَيْنِنَا وَاهْدِنَا سُبُلَ
السَّلَامِ وَنَجِّنَا مِنَ الظُّلُمَاتِ إِلَى النُّورِ وَجَنِّبْنَا الْفَوَاحِشَ مَا ظَهَرَ
مِنْهَا وَمَا بَطَنَ وَبَارِكْ لَنَا فِي أَسْمَاعِنَا وَأَبْصَارِنَا وَقُلُوبِنَا
وَأَزْوَاجِنَا وَذُرِّيَّاتِنَا وَتُبْ عَلَيْنَا إِنَّكَ أَنْتَ التَّوَّابُ الرَّحِيمُ
وَاجْعَلْنَا شَاكِرِينَ لِنِعَمِكَ مُثْنِينَ بِهَا عَلَيْكَ وَأَتِمَّهَا عَلَيْنَا

Allahumma alif bayna qulubina wa aslih dhat baynina wa ihdina subul as-salam wa najjina min az-zulumat ila an-nur wa janibna al-fawahish ma zahara minha wa ma batan, wa barik lana fi asma'ina wa absarina wa qulubina wa azwajina wa dhuriyyatina, wa tub 'alayna innaka anta at-tawwab ar-rahim wa i'jalna shakira li nimatik, muthna 'ala nimatik wa atmimha 'alayna.

Oh Allah, unite our hearts and settle our mutual affairs, guide us to the path of peace, save us from the darkness [of disbelief and confusion] to the light [of belief and understanding], keep us away from lewdness, the obvious and the hidden, bless our ears, eyes, hearts, spouses, and offspring, turn to us, surely you are the Oft-Returning, Merciful. Make us thankful for Your bounty, praising it, and completing it on us.

Source: Jami' at-Tirmidhi 3501

Story of Wisdom:

قال رسول الله صلّى الله عليه وسلّم: ال تناجشوا ولا
تحاسدوا ولا تباغضوا ولا تدابروا ولا يبع بعضكم على
بيع بعض وكونوا عباد الله إخوانا. المسلم المسلم من سلم
المسلمون من لسانه ويده. والمهاجر من هجر ما نهى الله عنه.

Qala rasool Allahi salla Allah 'alayhi wa sallam: "La tanajasho wa la tahasado wa la tabaghadu wa la tadabaru wa la yabi' ba'dukum 'ala bay'i ba'd wa kunu 'ibad Allah ikhwanan. Al-Muslim as-salim min salim al-Muslimoon min lisanhi wa yadih. Wa al-muhajir man hajara ma naha Allah 'anhu."

The Messenger of God, peace be upon him, said: "Do not undercut each other in transactions; do not bear grudges against one another; do not turn away from one another; do not outsell one another [in a way that harms the other]; and be, O God's servants, brothers [to one another]. A Muslim is the one from whose tongue and hands the Muslims are safe. And the emigrant (muhajir) is the one who refrains from what God has forbidden."

Source: Sahih al-Bukhari 6066

Dua for Success of Islamic Projects

اللّهمّ ال سهل إال ما جعلته سهال، وأنت تجعل الـحزن إذا شئت سهال

Allahumma la sahla illa ma ja'altahu sahla, wa 'anta taj'alul-hazna idha shi'ta sahla

O Allah, nothing is easy except what You have made easy. If You will, You can make the difficult easy.

Source: Sunan Ibn Majah 3241

Story of Wisdom:

إذ قال أصحاب الكهف والرقيم إذاوا على كهفهم يقولون
ربنا آتنا من لدنك رحمة وهيئ لنا من أمرنا رشدا

Idh qaaloo ashaabul-Kahfi war-Raqeemi idhaawaa 'alaa kahfihim yaqooloona Rabbanaaa aatinaa milladunka Rahmah wa hayyi' lanaa min amrinaa Rashada

64

When the companions of the cave and inscription said while residing in their cave, "Our Lord, give us from Yourself mercy and prepare for us from our affair right guidance."

Source: Qur'an (18:10)

Dua for Guidance for Non-Muslims

اللّٰهُمَّ اهدِني فيمَن هدَيتَ، وعَافِني فيمَن عَافَيتَ، وتوَلَّني
فيمَن تولَّيتَ، وبارِكْ لي فيمَا اعطَيتَ، وقِني شرَّ ما
قضَيتَ، فإنَّكَ تقضِي ولو يُقضَى عليكَ، إنّهُ لا يذِلُ مَن
والَيتَ، ولو يَعزُ مَن عادَيتَ، تبارَكتَ ربنَا وتعالَيتَ.

Allahumma ihdini feeman hadayt, wa 'aafini feeman 'aafayt, wa tawallani feeman tawallayt, wa barik li feema a'atayt, wa qini sharra ma qadayt, fa innaka taqdi wa la yuqda 'alayk, innahu la yadhillu man walaayt, wa la ya'izzu man 'aadayt, tabarakta rabbana wa ta'alayt.

O Allah, guide me among those You have guided, and grant me safety among those You have granted safety. Take me into Your charge among those You have taken into Your charge, and bless that which You have given me. Protect me from the evil You have decreed, for You decree, and nothing is decreed for You. He whom You befriend is not humiliated. And he who is your enemy is never exalted. O our Lord, You are blessed and exalted.

Source: Sunan Abu Dawood 5067

Story of Wisdom:

عَنْ أبي هرَيرَةَ، قالَ قالَ رَسُولُ اللّٰهِ صَلَّى اللّٰهُ علَيهِ
وسلَّمَ "الا إ الأَ خُبرُكُمْ بمَن حَرَّمَ علَيهِ النّارُ أوْ بمَنْ حَرَّمَ
النّارُ علَيهِ علَى كلّ هَيِّنٍ لَيّنٍ قرِيبٍ سَهْلٍ"

An abi Huraira, qala qala rasul Allahi salla Allahu 'alayhi wa sallam "ala ukhbirukum biman taharrama 'alayhi al-nar? 'aw biman taharramat al-naru 'alayh? 'ala kulli hayyin layyin qareeb sahl"

On the authority of Abu Hurairah, he said: The Messenger of Allah peace be upon him said, "Shall I not inform you for whom the Hellfire is forbidden? It is forbidden for every gentle, soft-hearted, close, and easygoing person."

Source: Sahih al-Bukhari 6464

Dua for Support in Community Service

اللّهَمّ إنّ نسألك الهدى والتقى والعفاف والغنى

Allahumma innā nasaluka al-hudā wa at-tuqā wa al-'afāf wa al-ghinā

O Allah, we ask You for guidance, piety, chastity and self-sufficiency.

Source: Sahih Muslim 2721

Story of Wisdom:

قال رسول الله صلّى الله عليه وسلّم: "أفضل الناس أنفعهم للناس"

Qāla rasūl Allahi salla Allahu 'alayh wa sallam: "afdhal al-nās anfa'uhum lil-nās"

The Messenger of Allah, may Allah bless him and grant him peace, said: "The best of people are those most beneficial to people."

Source: Sunan al-Dārimī 2346

Dua for Blessings in Charity and Alms

Dua for Seeking Increase in Wealth and Blessings

Arabic:

رَبَّنَا آتِنَا فِي الدُّنْيَا حَسَنَةً وَفِي الآخِرَةِ حَسَنَةً وَقِنَا عَذَابَ النَّارِ

Rabbana atina fi ad-dunya hasanatan wa fi al-akhirati hasanatan wa qina 'adhaban-nar

Our Lord, give us good in this world and good in the Hereafter, and protect us from the torment of the Fire.

Source: The Quran, Surah Al-Baqarah (2:201)

Story of Wisdom:

فِي الْحَدِيثِ - ,, مَا نَقَصَتْ صَدَقَةٌ مِنْ مَالٍ وَمَا زَادَ اللَّهُ عَبْدًا
بِعَفْوٍ إِلَّا عِزًّا، وَمَا تَوَاضَعَ أَحَدٌ لِلَّهِ إِلَّا رَفَعَهُ اللَّهُ،،

Wa fi al-hadith - "Ma naqasat sadaqatun min maalin, wa ma zaada Allahu
'abdan bi'afwin illa 'izzan, wa ma tawada'a ahadun lillahi illa rafa'ahu Allah."

And in the hadith - "Charity does not diminish wealth, and Allah does not
increase a servant (in his provision) due to his forgiving nature except in
honor, and no one humbles himself for Allah but Allah raises him (in status)."

Source: Sahih Muslim 2588.

Dua for Protection of Islamic Institutions

اللَّهُمَّ إِنِّي أَعُوذُ بِكَ مِنْ عَذَابِ الْقَبْرِ، وَأَعُوذُ بِكَ مِنْ عَذَابِ
فِتْنَةِ الْمَسِيحِ الدَّجَّالِ، وَأَعُوذُ بِكَ مِنْ فِتْنَةِ الْمَحْيَا
وَالْمَمَاتِ . اللَّهُمَّ إِنِّي أَعُوذُ بِكَ مِنَ الْمَأْثَمِ وَالْمَغْرَمِ

Allahumma inni a'udhu bika min 'adhabil-qabr, wa a'udhu bika min fitnatil-
masihid-dajjal, wa a'udhu bika min fitnatil-mahya wa al-mamat. Allahumma
inni a'udhu bika minal-ma'thami wal-maghram.

Oh Allah, I seek refuge with You from the torment of the grave, and I seek
refuge with You from the trial of the False Messiah, and I seek refuge with
You from the trials of life and death. Oh Allah, I seek refuge with You from
sin and heavy debt.

Source: Sunan Abi Dawood 5090

Story of Wisdom:

قال النَّبِيّ صلَّى اللهُ عليهِ وسلَّم: (ليس الشَّديدُ بالصرعة
، إنما الشَّديدُ الذي يملكُ نفسَه عند الغضب).

Qala an-Nabiyy salla Allahu 'alayhi wa sallam: (laysa ash-shadidu bis-sara'ah,
inama ash-shadidu alladhee yamliku nafsahu 'ind al-ghadab)

The Prophet, peace be upon him, said: "The strong man is not the one who can overpower others (in wrestling); rather, the strong man is the one who controls himself when he gets angry."

Source: Sahih al-Bukhari 6114

Chapter 7:
Navigating Life: Duas for Daily Challenges and Situations

Dua for Ease in Hardship

اللّٰهُمَّ رَحْمَتَكَ أَرْجُو فَلَا تَكِلْنِي إِلَى نَفْسِي طَرْفَةَ
عَيْنٍ، وَأَصْلِحْ لِي شَأْنِي كُلَّهُ ، لَا إِلَٰهَ إِلَّا أَنْتَ

Allahumma rahmataka arjoo fala takilnee ila nafsee tarfata ʿaynin, wa aslih lee shaʾnee kullahu, la ilaha illa ant

O Allah, I hope for Your Mercy. Do not leave me to myself even for the blinking of an eye, and correct all of my affairs. There is no god but You.

Source: Abu Dawood

Story of Wisdom:

قَالَ النَّبِيُّ صَلَّى اللهُ عَلَيْهِ وَسَلَّمَ: ,,إذا أراد اللهُ بعبدهِ
الخير عجّل لهُ العقوبةَ في الدنيا، وإذا أراد اللهُ بعبدهِ
الشر أمسك عنه بذنبهِ حتّى يوافيَ بهِ يوم القيامة''

Qala an-Nabi salla Allahu ʿalayhi wa sallam: "Idha arada Allahu bi ʿabdihi al-khair ʿajjala lahu al-ʿuqoobata fi al-dunya, wa idha arada Allahu bi ʿabdihi ash-sharr ʿamsaka ʿanhu bi dhambihi hatta yuwaffi bihi yawm al-qiyamah"

The Prophet (peace be upon him) said: "When Allah wants good for His servant, He hastens his punishment in this world, and when Allah wants evil for His servant, He withholds from him (the punishment for) his sin until He recompenses him for it on the Day of Resurrection."

Source: Tirmidhi

Dua for Trust in Allah's Plan

اللّٰهُمَّ لَكَ أَسْلَمْتُ، وَبِكَ آمَنْتُ، وَعَلَيْكَ تَوَكَّلْتُ، وَإِلَيْكَ أَنَبْتُ، وَبِكَ خَاصَمْتُ، اللّٰهُمَّ إِنِّي أَعُوذُ بِعِزَّتِكَ لَا إِلَهَ إِلَّا أَنْتَ أَنْ تُضِلَّنِي، أَنْتَ الْحَيُّ الَّذِي لَا يَمُوتُ، وَالْجِنُّ وَالْإِنْسُ يَمُوتُونَ

Allahumma laka aslamtu, wa bika amantu, wa 'alaika tawakkaltu, wa ilaika anabtu, wa bika khasamtu. Allahumma inni a'udhu bi'izzatika, la ilaha illa anta an tudillani. Anta al-Hayyul-ladhee la yamoot, wa al-jinnu wal-insu yamootoon.

O Allah, to You I have submitted, in You I have believed, in You I have placed my trust, to You I have turned, and with Your Aid I argue. O Allah, I seek refuge in Your Might, there is no deity but You, that You will mislead me. You are the Ever-Living who does not die, while the jinn and humans will die.

Source: Jami' at-Tirmidhi 3604

Story of Wisdom:

قَالَ اللّٰهُ تَعَالَى: إِنَّمَا أَمْرُهُ إِذَا أَرَادَ شَيْئًا أَنْ يَقُولَ لَهُ كُنْ فَيَكُونُ

Qaala Allahu Ta'ala: Innama amruhu iza arada shay'an an yaqula lahu kun fayakoon

Allah Almighty said: His command, when He intends a thing, is only that He says to it, "Be," and it is.

Source: Surah Ya-Sin 36:82

Dua for Protection from Envy

اللّٰهُمَّ إِنِّي أَعُوذُ بِكَ مِنَ الْبَرَصِ، وَالْجُنُونِ، وَالْجُذَامِ، وَمِنْ سَيِّئِ الْأَسْقَامِ

Allahumma inni a'udhu bika minal-barasi, wal-junooni, wal-judhaami, wa min sayyil-asqaami

O Allah, I seek refuge in You from leprosy, madness, elephantiasis, and from the worst of diseases.

Source: Sahih Muslim 2206

Story of Wisdom:

قَالَ رَسُوْلُ اللهِ صَلّى اللهُ عَلَيْهِ وَسَلّمَ ١١ لَا حَسَدَ إِلَّا فِيْ
اثْنَتَيْنِ رَجُلٌ آتَاهُ اللهُ مَالاً فَسَلّطَ عَلَى هَلَكَتِهِ فِي الْحَقِّ
وَرَجُلٌ آتَاهُ اللهُ حِكْمَةً فَهُوَ يَقْضِيْ بِهَا وَيُعَلِّمُهَا ١١.

Qala rasool Allahi salla Allahu alayhi wa sallam "La hasada illa fi ithnatayn,
rajulun atahu Allah malan fasullita ala halakatihi fil haqqi, wa rajulun atahu
Allahu hikmatan fahuwa yaqdee biha wayu'allimoha."

The Messenger of Allah said, "Envy is only justified in two cases: A man
whom Allah gives wealth, and he disposes of it rightfully, and a man to whom
Allah gives knowledge which he applies and teaches it."

Source: Sahih al-Bukhari 73

Dua for Relief from Debt

اللّهُمّ اكْفِنِيْ بِحَلَالِكَ عَنْ حَرَامِكَ، وَأَغْنِنِيْ بِفَضْلِكَ عَمّنْ سِوَاكَ

Allahumma ikfini bihalalika 'an haramika, wa aghnini bifadlika 'amman siwaka

Oh Allah, make Your lawful bounties sufficient for me so as to save me from
anything that is unlawful, and from Your grace, make me independent of all
others besides You.

Source: Jami` at-Tirmidhi 3563

Story of Wisdom:

وَقَالَ الْمَلِكُ إِنِّيْ أَرَى سَبْعَ بَقَرَاتٍ سِمَانٍ يَأْكُلُهُنّ سَبْعٌ
عِجَافٌ وَسَبْعَ سُنْبُلَاتٍ خُضْرٍ وَأُخَرَ يَابِسَاتٍ يَا أَيُّهَا الْمَلَأُ
أَفْتُوْنِيْ فِيْ رُؤْيَايَ إِنْ كُنْتُمْ لِلرُّؤْيَا تَعْبُرُوْنَ

Wa qala al-maliku inni ara sab'a baqaratin simanin ya'kuluhunna sab'un 'ijafun
wa sab'a sunbulatin khudrin wa ukhara yabisatin ya ayyuha al-mala'u aftuni fi
ru'yaya in kuntum lir-ru'ya ta'burun

The king (of Egypt) said, "Indeed, I see [in a dream] seven fat cows being
eaten by seven [that are] lean, and seven green spikes [of grain] and others

[that are] dry. O chiefs, explain to me my vision, if you should interpret visions."

Source: Qur'an 12:43

Dua for a Righteous Spouse

اللّٰهُمَّ إِنِّي أَسْأَلُكَ لِزَوْجِي خَيْرَهُ، وَأَعُوذُ بِكَ مِنْ شَرِّهِ

Allahumma inni as'aluka lizawji khayrah, wa a'udhu bika min sharrih

Oh Allah, I ask You for the goodness within my spouse, and I seek refuge in You from his/her evil.

Source: Abu Dawood 2160

Story of Wisdom:

قال رسول الله صلَّى الله عليه وسلَّم: (أفضل الدُّنيا المَرْأةُ الصَّالِحَةُ)

Qala Rasool Allahi salla Allah alayhi wa sallam: (Afdal al-dunya al-mar'atu al-salihah)

The Prophet Muhammad (peace be upon him) said: "The best thing in the world is a righteous woman."

Source: Sahih Muslim 2724

Dua for Blessings in the Home

اللّٰهُمَّ بارك لنا في بيوتنا، وأسعدنا في أهلنا، واجعل لنا من أموالنا نفعًا، وأصلح لنا ديننا الذي هو عصمة أمورنا، ودنيانا التي فيها معاشنا، وآخرتنا التي إليها معادنا، واجعل الحياة زيادة لنا في كل خير، والموت راحة لنا من كل شر.

Allahumma barik lana fi buyutina, wa as'adna fi ahlinna, wa ijal lana min amwalina naf'a, wa aslih lana dinana alladhee huwa 'ismatu umurina, wa dunyana allati feeha ma'ashuna, wa akhiratana allati ilayha ma'aduna, wa ijal al-hayata ziyadatan lana fi kulli khayr, wa al-mawta rahatan lana min kulli shar.

O Allah, bless us in our homes, and grant us happiness with our families, and make our wealth beneficial for us, and rectify for us our religion which is the safeguard of our affairs, and our world in which is our livelihood, and our hereafter to which is our return, and make life an increase for us in every goodness, and death a rest for us from every evil.

Source: Hisn al Muslim 69

Story of Wisdom:

عن أبي هريرة رضي الله عنه أن رسول الله صلّى الله عليه وسلّم قال: إن الله كتب الإحسان على كل شيء، فإذا قتلتم فأحسنوا القتلة، وإذا ذبحتم فأحسنوا الذبحة، وليحد أحدكم شفرته وليرح ذبيحته.

'An abi hurairata radi Allahu 'anhu 'an rasul Allahi salla Allahu 'alayhi wa sallam qaala: inna Allaha kataba al-ihsaana 'ala kulli shay'in, fa'ithaa qataltum fa'ahsinoo al-qatlata, wa'ithaa dhabahtum fa'ahsinoo al-dhabihata, walyuhid 'ahadukum shafaratahu walyurah dhabiyyatahu.

Narrated by Abu Hurairah, may Allah be pleased with him, that the Messenger of Allah, peace and blessings be upon him, said: Verily, Allah has prescribed excellence in all things. So if you kill, then kill well; and if you slaughter, then slaughter well. Let each one of you sharpen his blade and let him spare suffering to the animal he slaughters.

Source: Sahih Muslim 1955.

Dua for Keeping Family Together

اللهمَّ اجعل أولادي قرة عيني، واجعلهم الورثة الصالحين، واجعلهم من الذين يرثون الجنة، واجعلهم من الصادقين في قولهم وفعلهم، واجعلهم من الصابرين على بلائك، واجعلهم من الشاكرين لنعمائك، واجعلهم من الذين يتقونك في السرّ والعلن.

Allahumma ija'al awladi qurrata 'ayni, waija'alhum alwaritha assalihin, waija'alhum min alladhina yarithuna aljannata, waija'alhum min assadiqin fi qawlihim wafi'lihim, waija'alhum min assabirin 'ala bala'ik, waija'alhum min ashshakirin lina'imaik, waija'alhum min alladhina yattaqunak fi assirri wal'alani

Oh Allah, make my children the comfort of my eyes, and make them righteous successors, and make them among those who will inherit Paradise, and make them among those who are truthful in their words and actions, and make them among those who are patient in Your trials, and make them among those who are thankful for Your blessings, and make them among those who fear You in private and in public.

Source: Al-Sahifah al-Sajjadiyya Dua 25

Story of Wisdom:

قَالَتْ نَمْلَةٌ يَا أَيُّهَا النَّمْلُ ادْخُلُوا مَسَاكِنَكُمْ لَا يَحْطِمَنَّكُمْ سُلَيْمَانُ وَجُنُودُهُ وَهُمْ لَا يَشْعُرُونَ.

Qalat namlatun ya ayyuha alnamlu udkhuloo masakinakum la yahtimannakum sulaymanu wajunooduhu wahum la yash'uroon.

An ant said, "O ants, enter your homes that you not be crushed by Solomon and his soldiers while they perceive not."

Source: Surah An-Naml 27:18

Dua for Guidance in Making Decisions

اللَّهُمَّ لَا تَكِلْنِي إِلَى نَفْسِي طَرْفَةَ عَيْنٍ وَلَا أَقَلَّ مِنْ ذَلِكَ، اللَّهُمَّ أَصْلِحْ شَأْنِي كُلَّهُ، لَا إِلَهَ إِلَّا أَنْتَ

Allahumma la takilni ila nafsi tarfata ainin wa la aqalla min dhalik, Allahumma aslih sha'ni kullahu, la ilaha illa ant

Oh Allah, do not leave me to myself even for the blinking of an eye (i.e., a moment), and correct all my affairs. There is no god but You.

Source: Sunan Abi Dawud 5090

Story of Wisdom:

عَنْ أَبِي هُرَيْرَةَ، عَنِ النَّبِيِّ صَلَّى اللهُ عَلَيْهِ وَسَلَّمَ قَالَ: "مَنْ يُرِدِ اللهُ بِهِ خَيْرًا يُفَقِّهْ فِي الدِّينِ"

An abi hurairah, 'an al-nabi salla Allah 'alayh wa sallam qal: "man yurid allah bih khayr yufaqqih fi al-deen"

Abu Hurairah reported that the Prophet (peace be upon him) said: "If Allah intends good for someone, He grants him understanding in the religion."

Source: Sahih al-Bukhari 71

Dua for Barakah in Rizq (Provision)

اللَّهُمَّ بَارِكْ لِي فِيمَا رَزَقْتَنِي وَقِنِي شَرَّ مَا قَضَيْتَ

Allahumma barik lee feema razaqtanee waqini sharra ma qadayt

Oh Allah, bless me in what You have provided me and protect me from the evil of what You have decreed.

Source: Jami` at-Tirmidhi 3380

Story of Wisdom:

قَالَ رَسُولُ اللَّهِ صَلَّى اللهُ عَلَيهِ وسَلَّمَ ‘‘مَا مِنْ أَحَدٍ يَأْكُلُ طَعَامًا فَيَحْمَدُ اللَّهَ عَزَّ وَجَلَّ عَلَيْهِ إِلَّا كَفَّرَ اللَّهُ لَهُ مَا سَلَفَ مِنْ ذَنْبِهِ‘‘

Qala rasool Allahi salla Allah alaihi wa sallam "ma min ahad y'akulu ta`aman fayhamidu Allah `azza wa jalla `alayhi illa kaffara Allah lahu ma salaf min dhanbihi"

The Messenger of Allah said, "There is no one who eats a meal and then praises Allah, the Exalted and Majestic, for it, except that Allah forgives his previous sins."

Source: Sunan Ibn Majah 3287

Dua for Protection from Natural Disasters

اللَّهُمَّ إِنِّي أَعُوذُ بِكَ مِنَ الْبُخْلِ، وَأَعُوذُ بِكَ مِنَ الْفَقْرِ،
وَأَعُوذُ بِكَ مِنَ الْغَرَقِ، وَأَعُوذُ بِكَ مِنَ هَدْمِ الدِّيَارِ

Allahumma inni a'udhu bika min al-bukhl, wa a'udhu bika min al-faqr, wa a'udhu bika min

al-gharaq, wa a'udhu bika min hadm al-diyar

O Allah, I seek refuge with You from stinginess, poverty, drowning, and from the destruction of homes.

Source: Jami` at-Tirmidhi 3609

Story of Wisdom:

وَمَا أَرْسَلْنَا فِي قَرْيَةٍ مِن نَبِيٍّ إِلَّا أَخَذْنَا أَهْلَهَا
بِالْبَأْسَاءِ وَالضَّرَّاءِ لَعَلَّهُمْ يَضَّرَّعُونَ

Wa ma arsalna fi qaryatin min nabiyyin illa akhadhna ahlahab-al-ba'sa'i wa al-darra'i la'allahum yaddarra'oon

And We sent no Prophet to any town but We seized its people with suffering and adversity, that they might humble themselves.

Source: Qur'an 7:94

Dua for Healing Broken Relationships

اللَّهُمَّ أَلِّفْ بَيْنَ قُلُوبِنَا، وَأَصْلِحْ ذَاتَ بَيْنِنَا، وَاهْدِنَا
سُبُلَ السَّلَامِ، وَنَجِّنَا مِنَ الظُّلُمَاتِ إِلَى النُّورِ

Allahumma alif bayna qulubina, wa aslih dhat baynina, wahdina subul al-salam, wanajjina min al-zulumati ila al-noor

O Allah, reconcile our hearts, amend our relations, guide us to the paths of peace, and save us from the darkness to the light.

Source: Sunan Abi Dawood 4919

Story of Wisdom:

قَالَ رَسُولُ اللهِ صَلَّى اللهُ عَلَيْهِ وسَلَّمَ: لَا يَفْرِكْ
مُؤْمِنٌ مُؤْمِنَةً إِنْ كَرِهَ مِنْهَا خُلُقًا رَضِيَ مِنْهَا آخَرَ

Qala rasool allah salla Allah alayhi wa sallam: la yufrak muminun muminan in karih minha khuluqa radi minha akhar

The Prophet Muhammad (peace be upon him) said: A believer should not hate a fellow believer. If he dislikes one characteristic in him, he should be pleased with another.

Source: Sahih Muslim 2165

Dua for Finding Lost Items

اللّٰهُمَّ رَادَّ الضَّالَّةِ وَهَادِيَ الضَّالَّةِ أَنْتَ تَهْدِي مِنَ الضَّلَالَةِ رُدَّ عَلَيَّ
ضَالَّتِي بِقُدْرَتِكَ وَسُلْطَانِكَ فَإِنَّهَا مِنْ فَضْلِكَ وَعَطَائِكَ

Allahumma radda-ddallati wa-hadiya-ddallati anta tahdi mina-ddallati rudda alayya dallati bi-qudratika wa sultanika fa-innaha min fadlika wa'ataaika

O Allah, the Returner of the lost, and the Guide of the lost, You guide the lost. Return my lost item to me by Your power and Your rule, for it is from Your bounty and Your gift.

Source: Hisnul Muslim (Fortress of the Muslim)

Story of Wisdom:

قَالَ رَجُلٌ مِنَ الْمُهَاجِرِينَ لِرَجُلٍ مِنَ الْأَنْصَارِ فِي شِجَارٍ بَيْنَهُمَا: يَا
لَلْأَنْصَارِ، وَقَالَ الْأَنْصَارِيُّ: يَا لَلْمُهَاجِرِ. فَجَاءَ النَّبِيُّ صَلَّى اللّٰهُ
عَلَيْهِ وَسَلَّمَ وَقَدْ أُخْبِرَ بِذَلِكَ فَقَالَ: مَا بَالُ دَعْوَى الْجَاهِلِيَّةِ؟ قَالُوا:
يَا رَسُولَ اللّٰهِ، قَالَ مُهَاجِرٌ فِي شِجَارِهِ لِأَنْصَارِيٍّ: يَا لَلْأَنْصَارِ،
وَقَالَ الْأَنْصَارِيُّ: يَا لَلْمُهَاجِرِ. فَقَالَ: دَعُوهَا فَإِنَّهَا مُنْتِنَةٌ

Qala rajulun minal-muhajirina li-rajulin minal-ansari fi shijaarin baynahuma: ya la-ansara, wa qala al-ansariyyu: ya la-muhajira. Faja'a an-nabiyu sallallahu alayhi wa sallam wa qad ukhbir bi-dhalika faqala: ma balu da'wa al-jahiliyyati? Qalu: ya Rasulallah, qala muhajirun fi shijaarihi li-ansariyyin: ya la-ansara, wa qala al-ansariyyu: ya la-muhajira. Faqala: da'uha fa-innaha muntinah

A man from the emigrants said to a man from the Ansar (in the course of an argument between them): "O the Ansar!" And the Ansari said: "O the Emigrants!" When the Prophet (PBUH) was informed about this, he said: "What is this call of ignorance?" They said: "O Allah's Messenger, a man from the emigrants said in his argument to the Ansari: 'O the Ansar!' and the Ansari said: 'O the Emigrants!'" The Prophet said: "Leave it (this call) as it is detestable."

Source: Sahih al-Bukhari 6158

Dua for Success in Business

اَللَّهُمَّ إِنِّ أَسْأَلُكَ عِلْمًا نَافِعًا ،وَ رِزْقًا طَيِّبًا، وَعَمَلًا مُتَقَبَّلًا

Allahumma inni as'aluka 'ilman nafi'an, wa rizqan tayyiban, wa 'amalan mutaqabbalan

Oh Allah, I ask you for knowledge that is beneficial, a good provision and deeds that will be accepted.

Source: Jami` at-Tirmidhi 3599

Story of Wisdom:

قال رسول الله صلّى الله عليه وسلّم: إن الله
يحب اذا عمل أحدكم عملا أن يتقنه

Qaala rasool Allahi salla Allahu 'alayhi wa sallam: 'inna Allah yuhibbu idha 'amila ahadukum 'amalan 'an yatqinahu

The Prophet Muhammad (peace be upon him) said: "Verily, Allah loves when one of you performs a job, that he does it with perfection."

Source: Sahih Al Bukhari 3466

Chapter 8:
Reflective Times: Duas for
Different Times of Day

Dua for Blessing in Early Morning

اللَّهُمَّ بِكَ أَصْبَحْنَا، وَبِكَ أَمْسَيْنَا، وَبِكَ
نَحْيَا، وَبِكَ نَمُوتُ، وَإِلَيْكَ النُّشُورُ

Allahumma bika asbahna, wa bika amsayna, wa bika nahya, wa bika namutu, wa ilayka an-nushoor.

Oh Allah, with You we enter the morning, and with You we enter the evening, by You we live, and by You we die, and to You is the Resurrection.

Source: Sahih Al-Bukhari 6324, Sahih Muslim 2711

Story of Wisdom:

وَالْعَصْرِ

إِنَّ الْاِنْسَانَ لَفِي خُسْرٍ

إِلَّا الَّذِينَ آمَنُوا وَعَمِلُوا الصَّالِحَاتِ وَتَوَاصَوْا بِالْحَقِّ وَتَوَاصَوْا بِالصَّبْرِ

Wa al-'asr, inna al-insana lafi khusr, illa allatheena amanoo wa 'amiloo as-salihat wa tawasaw bil-haqqi wa tawasaw bis-sabr

By time, indeed, mankind is in loss, except for those who have believed and done righteous deeds and advised each other to truth and advised each other to patience.

Source: Holy Qur'an, Surah Al-Asr (103:1-3)

Dua for Midday and Its Challenges

اللَّهُمَّ بَيِّضْ وَجهِي عَلى الصَّلاةِ عَليكَ وَلا تُسَوِّد وَجهِي بِمَعصِيَتِكَ،
اللَّهُمَّ فاشغِلنِي بِالخَيراتِ دُونَ السَّيِّئاتِ، حاجَتِكَ
وَبِالطاعاتِ دُونَ المَعاصِي، وَبِالمُواظَبَةِ عَلى الصَّلاةِ وَالسَّلامِ
عَلى مُحَمدٍ وَآلِ مُحَمدٍ ، وَلا تَجعَلنِي مِنَ الغافِلِينَ

Allahumma bayyid wajhi bisalah alayk wa la tusawwid wajhi bima'siyatika,
Allahumma fashghilni bilkhayrati dunas sayyi'ati, wabitta'ati dunal ma'asi,
wabilmuazibati 'ala salati was salami 'ala Muhammadin wa ali Muhammad, wa
la taj'alni min al ghafilin

O Allah, brighten my face with prayer for you and do not darken my face
with disobedience towards you. O Allah, occupy me with good deeds instead
of bad ones, with acts of obedience instead of transgressions, and with
being steadfast in prayer and peace upon Muhammad and the family of
Muhammad, and do not make me among the heedless.

Source: Imam Sajjad's Sahifa Sajjadiya (Dua 43)

Story of Wisdom:

حَدَّثَنا الأصمَعِي عَنِ الأزهَرِي عَنِ الزهرِي عَن عُروةَ بنِ الزبيرِ عَن عائشةَ
رَضِي اللهُ عنها قالَت: كانَ النَّبِيّ صَلّى اللهُ عليهِ وَسَلَّم يَقُولُ في
دعائِه: اللَّهُمَّ إِنِّي أعُوذُ بكَ مِن العَمَلِ الَّذِي لا يَرفَع وَمِنَ القَلبِ الَّذِي
لا يَخشى وَمِنَ النَّفسِ الَّتِي لا تَشبَع وَمِنَ الدعاءِ الَّذِي لا يُسمَع

Hadathana al-'asma'i 'an al-'azhari 'an al-zuhri 'an 'uruwah ibn al-zubayr 'an
'a'ishah radi allahu 'anha qalat: kan al-nabi salla allahu 'alayhi wa sallam yaqul
fi da'wah: allahumma inni a'udhu bika min al-'amal alladhi la yarfa' wamin
al-qalb alladhi la yakhsha wamin al-nafs allati la tashba' wamin al-du'a' alladhi
la yusma'

Narrated by Al-Asma'i from Al-Azhari from Al-Zuhri from Urwah Ibn Al-
Zubayr from Aisha, may Allah be pleased with her, who said: The Prophet,
peace and blessings be upon him, used to say in his supplication: "O Allah, I
seek refuge in You from deeds that do not elevate, from a heart that does not
fear, from a soul that is never satisfied, and from a supplication that is not
heard."

Source: Sahih Al-Bukhari 6369

Dua for Afternoon - Reflection and Gratitude

اللَّهُمَّ بك أصبحنا، وبك أمسينا، وبك
نحيا، وبك نموت، وإليك النُّشور

Allahumma bika asbahna, wa bika amsayna, wa bika nahya, wa bika namoot, wa ilayka an-nushoor.

Oh Allah, with You we enter the morning, and with You we enter the evening, with You we live and with You we die, and to You is the resurrection.

Source: Sunan Abi Dawood 5068

Story of Wisdom:

قال رجُلٌ للنبيِّ صلَّى الله عليه وسلم أرأيتَ إن أيَّامِي
ضيَّقتْ عليَّ فلم أدرِكْ أن أصومَ إلَّا ثلاثَةَ أيامٍ فأيُّ
الشَّهرِ أصومُ قال "أوَّلَ الشَّهرِ ووسَطَهُ وآخِرَهُ".

Qaala rajulun lin-nabiyyi sallAllahu 'alayhi wa sallam a-ra'ayta in ayyaamiy dayyaqat 'alayya falam adrik an asooma illa thalaathata ayyaamin fa-ayyu ash-shahri asoomuhaa qaala "awwala ash-shahri wa wasatahu wa akhirahu".

A man said to the Prophet, peace be upon him, "What if my days are restricted and I can only fast for three days. Which days of the month should I fast?" He replied "The beginning of the month, the middle and the end."

Source: Sahih Al-Bukhari 1985

Dua for Evening Protection and Peace

بسمِ اللهِ الذي لا يَضُرُّ مَعَ اسْمِهِ شيءٌ في الأرضِ
ولا في السَّماءِ وهُوَ السَّميعُ العَليمُ

Bismillahilladhee la yadurru ma'asmihi shay'un fil ardi wa la fis samaa'i wa huwa assamee'ul 'aleem

In the name of Allah, with Whose name nothing on earth or in heaven can harm, and He is the All-Hearing, the All-Knowing.

Source: Tirmidhi

Story of Wisdom:

قَالَ رَسُولُ اللّٰهِ صَلّى اللّٰه عليه وسلّم "إِ, ثَلَاثَةٌ مَنْ كُنَّ
فِيهِ وَجَدَ بِهِنّ حَلَاوَةَ الإِيمَانِ أَنْ يَكُونَ اللّٰهَ وَرَسُولُهُ أَحَبّ
إِلَيْهِ مِمَّا سِوَاهُمَا، وَأَنْ يُحِبّ الْمَرْءَ لَا يُحِبّهُ إِلّا لِلّٰهِ، وَأَنْ يَكْرَهَ
أَنْ يَعُودَ فِي الْكُفْرِ كَمَا يَكْرَهُ أَنْ يُلْقَى فِي النَّارِ [.'']

Qala rasoolullahi salla Allahu alayhi wa sallam "thalathatun man kunna feehi wajada bihinna halawata al-eemani. An yakuna Allahu wa rasooluhu ahabba ilayhi mimma siwahuma, wa an yuhibba al-mar'a la yuhibbuhu illa lillah, wa an yakrah an ya'ooda fee al-kufr kama yakrah an yulqa fee an-nar."

The Prophet Muhammad (peace be upon him) said: "Three things bring about the sweetness of faith: that Allah and His Messenger are more beloved to him than anything else; that he loves a person solely for the sake of Allah; and that he abhors returning to disbelief as much as he abhors being cast into fire."

Source: Sahih Bukhari and Muslim

Dua for Night - Forgiveness and Mercy

اللّٰهُمّ أَنْتَ رَبِّي لَا إِلٰهَ إِلّا أَنْتَ، خَلَقْتَنِي وَأَنَا عَبْدُكَ وَأَنَا عَلى عَهْدِكَ
وَوَعْدِكَ مَا اسْتَطَعْتَ، أَعُوذُ بِكَ مِنْ شَرِّ مَا صَنَعْتُ، أَبُوءُ لَكَ بِنِعْمَتِكَ
عَلَيّ وَأَبُوءُ بِذَنْبِي فَاغْفِرْ لِي فَإِنّهُ لَا يَغْفِرُ الذّنُوبَ إِلّا أَنْتَ

Allahumma anta Rabbi la ilaha illa anta, khalaqtani wa ana abduka, wa ana 'ala 'ahdika wa wa'dika mastata'tu, a'udhu bika min sharri ma sana'tu, abu'u Laka bini'matika 'alaiya, wa abu'u Laka bidhanbi faghfirli fainnahu la yaghfiru adh-dhunuba illa anta

O Allah! You are my Lord! None has the right to be worshipped but You. You created me and I am Your servant, and I abide to Your covenant and promise as best I can, I take refuge in You from the evil of which I committed. I acknowledge Your favor upon me and I acknowledge my sin, so forgive me, for verily none can forgive sin but You.

Source: Sahih al-Bukhari 6306

Story of Wisdom:

قال رجل للنبيِّ صلَّى الله عليه وسلَّم: أوصني،
قال: ال تغضب، فردّد مرارا، قال: ال تغضب

Qala rajulun lin-nabiyyi, sallallahu 'alayhi wa sallam: Ausini, qala: La taghdab, faraddada marraran, qala: La taghdab

A man said to the Prophet, peace be upon him: Advise me! The Prophet said, Do not become angry and furious. The man asked (the same) again and again, and the Prophet said in each case, Do not become angry and furious.

Source: Sahih al-Bukhari 6116

Dua for Tahajjud - Seeking Closeness to Allah

اللَّهُمَّ بِكَ أَحْيَا وَبِكَ أَمُوتُ وَإِلَيْكَ النُّشُورُ

Allahumma bika ahyaa wa bika amootu wa ilayka an-nushoor.

Oh Allah, with Your name I live, with Your name I die and to You is the resurrection.

Source: Sahih al-Bukhari 6312

Story of Wisdom:

قال رَسُولُ اللَّهِ صلَّى الله عليه وسلَّم: إنَّ اللَّهَ
يُحِبُّ إذَا عَمِلَ أَحَدُكُمْ عَمَلًا أَنْ يُتْقِنَهُ

Qala rasoolu Allahi salla Allahu 'alayhi wa sallam: "Inna Allah yuhibbu idha 'amila ahadukum 'amalan an yutqinahu".

The Messenger of Allah (peace be upon him) said, "Verily, Allah loves when one of you undertakes a task, he performs it with excellence.

Source: Sunan al-Bayhaqi 2135

Dua for Rainy Days and Thunderstorms

اَللّٰهُمَّ أَصْلِحْ لِي دِينِي الَّذِي هُوَ عِصْمَةُ أَمْرِي، وَأَصْلِحْ لِي دُنْيَايَ
الَّتِي فِيهَا مَعَاشِي، وَأَصْلِحْ لِي آخِرَتِي الَّتِي فِيهَا مَعَادِي، وَاجْعَلِ
الْحَيَاةَ زِيَادَةً لِي فِي كُلِّ خَيْرٍ، وَاجْعَلِ الْمَوْتَ رَاحَةً لِي مِنْ كُلِّ شَرٍّ

Allahumma aslih li deeni alladhee huwa 'ismatu amree, wa aslih li dunyaya
allatee feeha ma'ashi, wa aslih li akhirati allatee feeha ma'adi. waj'alil hayata
ziadatan li fee kulli khair, waj'alil mawta rahatan li min kulli shar.

O Allah, make my religion, which is my fortress, secure for me. Make my
world life, in which is my livelihood, good for me. Make my Hereafter, which
is my return, good for me. Make life an increase for me in every goodness, and
make death a comfort for me from every evil.

Source: Sahih Muslim 2720

Story of Wisdom:

عَنْ أَبِي هُرَيْرَةَ رَضِيَ اللّٰهُ عَنْهُ قَالَ: قَالَ رَسُولُ اللّٰهِ صَلَّى اللّٰهُ
عَلَيْهِ وَسَلَّمَ: ,, مَنْ يُرِدِ اللّٰهُ بِهِ خَيْرًا يُفَقِّهْهُ فِي الدِّينِ ,,

'An Abi Hurayrata Radiyallahu 'Anhu Qala: Qala Rasulullah Sallallahu 'Alayhi
wa Sallam: "Man Yuridi Allah Bihi Khairan Yufaqqihhu fi Ad-Deen."

Narrated by Abu Huraira, may Allah be pleased with him, he said: The
Messenger of Allah, peace and blessings upon him, said: "If Allah intends
good for someone, then he grants him understanding in the religion."

Source: Sahih al-Bukhari 71.

Dua for Seeing a New Moon

اللّٰهُمَّ أَهِلَّهُ عَلَيْنَا بِالْأَمْنِ وَالْإِيمَانِ وَالسَّلَامَةِ وَالْإِسْلَامِ
وَالْعَافِيَةِ مَا تُحِبُّ وَتَرْضَى رَبَّنَا وَرَبُّكَ اللّٰهُ

Allahumma ahillahu 'alayna bil-amni wal-imani, wassalamati wal-Islam, wal-
'afiyati ma tuhibbu wa tardha. Rabbuna wa rabbuk Allah.

Oh Allah, bring it to us with security and faith, safety and Islam, and in a
state of wellbeing in which You are pleased. Our Lord and your Lord is Allah.

Source: Sunan Abu Dawood 1760

Story of Wisdom:

قال رسول الله صلّى الله عليه وسلّم: لا
تسبّوا الدهر، فإنّ الله هو الدهر

Qala rasool Allahi salla Allah 'alayh wa sallam: "La tasubbu ad-dahr, fa'inn Allah huwa ad-dahr"

The Prophet Muhammad (peace be upon him) said: "Do not revile time, for Allah is time."

Source: Sahih Muslim 5826

Dua for Friday - Blessings and Good Deeds

اللّهمّ صلّ وسلّم على نبيّنا محمد، وأغفر لنا
ولوالدينا وللمؤمنين يوم يقوم الحساب

Allahumma salli wa sallim 'ala nabiyyina Muhammad, wa'ghfir lana wa liwalidayna wa lil-mu'mineen yawma yaqoomu al-hisab

Oh Allah, bless and grant peace upon our Prophet Muhammad, and forgive us, our parents, and the believers on the Day of Reckoning.

Source: Tirmidhi 4857

Story of Wisdom:

إذ قال له ربّه أسلمْ قال أسلمتُ لربّ العالمين

Ith Qala Lahu Rabbuhu Aslim, Qala Aslamtu Li-Rabbi Al-'Alamin

When his Lord said to him, "Submit", he said "I have submitted [in Islam] to the Lord of the Worlds."

Source: Qur'an 2:131

Dua for Laylatul Qadr (The Night of Decree)

اللّهمّ إنّك عفوٌّ تحبّ العفو فأعْفُ عنّي

Allahumma innaka 'afuwwun tuhibbul 'afwa fa'fu 'anni

Oh Allah, You are the One Who pardons greatly, and loves to pardon, so pardon me.

Source: Tirmidhi 3513

Story of Wisdom:

وَإِذَا سَأَلَكَ عِبَادِي عَنِّي فَإِنِّي قَرِيبٌ أُجِيبُ دَعْوَةَ الدَّاعِ إِذَا دَعَانِ فَلْيَسْتَجِيبُوا لِي وَلْيُؤْمِنُوا بِي لَعَلَّهُمْ يَرْشُدُونَ

Wa idha sa'alaka 'ibadi 'anni fa'inni qareeb. Ujeebu da'watad-da'i idha da'an. Fal yastajeebu li wal yu'minu bi la'allahum yarshudoon

And when My servants ask you, [O Muhammad], concerning Me - indeed I am near. I respond to the invocation of the supplicant when he calls upon Me. So let them respond to Me [by obedience] and believe in Me that they may be [rightly] guided.

Source: The Holy Qur'an, Surah Al-Baqara (2:186)

Dua for Eid Celebrations

اللَّهُمَّ أهلَ الكبرياءِ والعظمةِ وأهلَ الجودِ والجبروتِ وأهلَ العفوِ والرحمةِ وأهلَ التقوى والمغفرةِ

أسألكَ بحقِّ هذا اليومِ الذي جعلتَهُ للمسلمينَ عيداً ولمحمَّدٍ صلَّى اللهُ عليهِ وسلَّمَ شرفاً ومزيداً أن تصلِّيَ على محمَّدٍ وعلى آلِ محمَّدٍ وأن تدخلني في كلِّ خيرٍ أدخلتَ فيهِ محمداً وآلَ محمدٍ وأن تخرجني من كلِّ سوءٍ أخرجتَ منهُ محمداً وآلَ محمَّدٍ صلَّى اللهُ عليهِ وسلَّمَ أنتَ القادرُ وبكَ أستعينَ

Allahumma ahlal-kibriyaa'i wal-'adhmah, wa ahlal-joodi wal-jabaroot, wa ahlal-afwi war-rahmah, wa ahlattaqwa wal-maghfirah

As'aluka bihaqqi haathal-yawm allathi ja'altahu lil-musalmeena 'eedan wa li-Muhammadin, sallallahu 'alayhi wa sallam, sharafan wa mazidan, an tusalli 'ala Muhammadin wa 'ala aali Muhammad, wa an tudkhilani fee kulli khayrin adkhalta feehi Muhammadan wa ala Muhammad, wa an tukhrijani min kulli sooin akhrajta minhu Muhammadan wa ala Muhammad sallallahu 'alayhi wa sallam. Anta al-Qadir wa bika asta'een.

O Allah! Lord of Supreme Majesty and Greatness, Lord of Honor and Power, Lord of Mercy and Forgiveness, Lord of Piety and Pardon, I ask You by the virtue of this day, which You have chosen as a festival for the Muslims and a source of dignity and increase for Muhammad, may peace be upon him, that You send blessings upon Muhammad and his family, and admit me into all the good in which You admitted Muhammad and his family, and extricate me from all the evil from which You freed Muhammad and his family. You are the Omnipotent, and I seek help only from You.

Source: Al-Tabarani in Al-Mu'jam Al-Kabir 7845

Story of Wisdom:

قَالَ رَسُولُ اللَّهِ صَلَّى اللهُ عليهِ وسَلَّمَ "لَا
يَشْكُرُ اللَّهَ مَنْ لَا يَشْكُرُ النَّاسَ"

Qāla rasūlullāhi salla Allahu 'alayh wa sallam "lā yashkurullāha man lā yashkuru an-nāsa."

The Messenger of Allah, Peace Be Upon Him, said: "He who does not thank people, does not thank Allah."

Source: Sunan Abi Dawood 4811

Dua for Entering a New Islamic Year

اللَّهُمَّ أَدْخِلْ عَلَيْنَا بِهَذِهِ السَّنَةِ الْجَدِيدَةِ الْعَافِيَةَ وَالإِيمَانَ
وَالسَّلَامَةَ وَالإِسْلَامَ وَرِضْوَانَكَ الْكَامِلَ وَعَافِيَةً مِنْ كُلِّ بَلِيَّةٍ

Allahumma adkhil 'alayna bihadhihissanatil jadidati al'afiyata wal-imana was-salamat wal-islaama wa ridwana-ka al-kamila wa 'afiyatan min kulli baliyyah

O Allah, with this new year, bring us health, faith, safety, Islam, your complete pleasure, and protection from all calamities.

Source: Al-Mu'jam al-Awsat 6236

Story of Wisdom:

قال رسول الله صلى الله عليه وسلم "إن من أفضل أيامكم يوم الجمعة فأكثروا عليّ من الصلاة فيه فإن صلاتكم معروضة عليّ". قالوا كيف تعرض صلاتنا عليك وقد أرمت. قال "إن الله حرّم على الأرض أن تأكل أجساد الأنبياء فنبي الله حي يرزق".

Qala rasoolullahi salla allahu alayhi wa sallam "Inna min afdal ayyamikum yawm al-jumu'ati fa'akthiru 'alayya mina-salati fihi fa'innna salatakum ma'rudhatun 'alayya". Qaloo kayfa tu'radhu salatuna 'alayka wa qad arimta. Qala "Inna Allah harrama 'ala al-ardi an ta'kula ajsad al-anbiyai fa nabiyyullahi hayyun yurzaqu."

The Messenger of Allah said, "Among the best of your days is Friday. On that day, increase your prayers upon me, for your prayers are displayed before me." They asked, "How can our prayers be displayed to you when your body has returned to the earth?" He replied, "Indeed, Allah has forbidden the earth to consume the bodies of the Prophets. The Prophet of Allah is alive and provided for."

Source: Sunan Abi Dawood 1047.

Dua for the Change of Seasons

اللهم اجعلنا من أوليائك الصالحين، الذين يتألقون بنور الإيمان في كل فصول الحياة، الذين يتجددون مع تجدد الأيام والليالي، اللهم اجعلنا من الصابرين في الشتاء والشاكرين في الصيف، الذين يستقبلون الربيع بالتسبيح والخريف بالتوبة والاستغفار، اللهم أعطنا خير ما في كل موسم وأكفنا شرها. آمين

Allahumma ij'alna min awliya'ika al-salihin, alladhina yata'allaquna binur al-iman fi kulli fusul al-hayat, alladhina yatatajaddaduna ma'a tajdid al-ayam wa al-layali, Allahumma ij'alna min al-sabirin fi al-shita' wa al-shakirin fi al-sayf, alladhina yastaqbiluna al-rabia' bi-al-tasbih wa al-kharif bi-al-tawba wa al-istighfar, Allahumma a'tina khair ma fi kulli mawsim wa akfina sharrah. Ameen

O Allah, make us among Your righteous allies, who shine with the light of faith in all seasons of life, who renew themselves with the renewal of days and nights, O Allah, make us among those who are patient in winter and thankful in summer, who welcome spring with praise and autumn with repentance and seeking forgiveness, O Allah, give us the best of what is in every season and protect us from its harm. Amen.

Source: Common Dua in the Muslim community

Story of Wisdom:

قال رسول الله صلّى الله عليه وسلّم : مثل الّذي يذكر
ربّه والّذي ال يذكر ربّه كمثل الحيّ والميّت

Qala rasul Allah salla Allah 'alaih wa sallam : "mathal allathi yadhkur rabbah wa allathi la yadhkur rabbahu ka mathal al-hayy wa al-mayit."

The Messenger of Allah (peace be upon him) said: "The example of the one who remembers his Lord, compared to the one who does not, is that of the living compared to the dead."

Source: Sahih al-Bukhari 6407

Chapter 9:
Spiritual Support: Duas for
Religious Obligations

Dua for Purification - Wudu and Ghusl

بِسْمِ اللهِ الرَّحْمَنِ الرَّحِيمِ اَللّهُمَّ اجْعَلْنِي مِنَ التَّوَّابِينَ وَاجْعَلْنِي مِنَ الْمُتَطَهِّرِينَ

Bismillah al-Rahman al-Rahim, Allahumma aj'alni mina at-tawwabina wa aj'alni min al-mutatahhirin

In the name of Allah, the Most Gracious, the Most Merciful. O Allah, make me among those who turn in repentance and make me among those who purify themselves.

Source: Sunan Ibn Majah 282.

Story of Wisdom:

وَقَالَ رَبُّكُمُ ادْعُونِي أَسْتَجِبْ لَكُمْ إِنَّ الَّذِينَ يَسْتَكْبِرُونَ عَنْ عِبَادَتِي سَيَدْخُلُونَ جَهَنَّمَ دَاخِرِينَ

Wa qala rabbukumud'ooni astajib lakum. Inn alladhina yastakbiroona 'an 'ibadati sayadkhuluna jahannama dakhireen

Your Lord says, 'Call upon Me, I will respond to you. Indeed, those who disdain My worship will enter Hell in disgrace.

Source: Qur'an 40:60

Dua for Entering and Leaving the Prayer Area

بِسْمِ اللهِ، وَالصَّلَاةُ وَالسَّلَامُ عَلَى رَسُولِ اللهِ، اللّهُمَّ اغْفِرْ لِي ذُنُوبِي وَاجْعَلْ خَيْرَ أَعْمَالِي خَوَاتِيمَهَا وَخَيْرَ أَيَّامِي يَوْمَ ألْقَاكَ فِيهِ.

Bismillahi, was-salatu was-salamu 'ala rasulillah, allahumma ighfir li dhunubi wa aj'al khaira a'amali khawatimaha wa khaira ayyami yawma alqaaka feeh.

In the name of Allah, and prayers and peace be upon the Messenger of Allah. O Allah, forgive my sins and make the best of my deeds the last ones and the best of my days the day I meet you.

Source: Al-Jami` at-Tirmidhi 3445

Story of Wisdom:

أَتَاهُ الْمَلَكُ فَقَالَ: اقْرَأْ, قَالَ: مَا أَنَا بِقَارِئٍ, قَالَ: فَأَخَذَنِي فَغَطَّنِي
حَتَّى بَلَغَ مِنِّي الْجَهْدُ, ثُمَّ أَرْسَلَنِي فَقَالَ: اقْرَأْ. قَالَ: فَمَا أَنَا بِقَارِئٍ,
فَأَخَذَنِي فَغَطَّنِي الثَّانِيَةَ حَتَّى بَلَغَ مِنِّي الْجَهْدُ، ثُمَّ أَرْسَلَنِي
فَأَخَذَنِي فَغَطَّنِي الثَّالِثَةَ ,قَالَ: اقْرَأْ. قَالَ: مَا أَنَا بِقَارِئٍ.
فَأَخَذَنِي فَغَطَّنِي الثَّالِثَةَ. فَلَمَّا بَلَغَ مِنِّي الْجَهْدُ أَرْسَلَنِي فَقَالَ: اقْرَأْ بِاسْمِ رَبِّكَ الَّذِي خَلَقَ.

Atahu al-malaku faqal: iqra. Qal: ma ana biqari. Qal: fa'akhadhani faghattani hatta balagha minni al-jahd, thumma arsalani faqal: iqra. Qal: fa ma ana biqari. Fa'akhadhani faghattani al-thaniyata hatta balagha minni al-jahd, thumma arsalani faqal: iqra. Qal: ma ana biqari. Fa'akhadhani faghattani al-thalithata. Fa lamma balagha minni al-jahd arsalani faqal: iqra bismi rabbika alladhee khalaq.

The angel came to him and said, "Read." He said, "I am not a reader." The angel grabbed him and enveloped him until he reached his limit, then let him go and said, "Read." He said, "I am not a reader." The angel grabbed him a second time until he reached his limit, then let him go and said, "Read." He said, "I am not a reader." The angel grabbed him a third time. When he reached his limit, the angel let him go and said, "Read in the name of your Lord who created."

Source: Sahih al-Bukhari 3

Dua for Concentration in Salah

اللَّهُمَّ إِنِّي أَعُوذُ بِكَ مِنْ زَوَالِ نِعْمَتِكَ, وَتَحَوُّلِ
عَافِيَتِكَ وَفُجَاءَةِ نِقْمَتِكَ وَجَمِيعِ سَخَطِكَ

Allahumma inni a'udhubika min zawali ni'matika, wa tahawwuli 'afiyatika, wa fuja'ati niqmatika wa jamee'i sa-khatika

91

O Allah, I seek refuge with You from the decline of Your bounties, the removal of Your protection, the sudden onset of Your punishment, and from all that displeases You.

Source: Sahih Muslim, 2726

Story of Wisdom:

وقد أخبرنا عن أبي سعيد الخدري رضي الله عنه قال: قال النبيّ
صلّى الله عليه وسلّم: "كيف أنعم وقد اتّخذ صاحب القرن القرن
فهو ينفخ فيه، قال: كأن رأسه جبل". قال: فقالوا: يا
رسول الله، فما تأمرنا؟ قال: "كونوا على بصيرة، واصبروا".

Wa qad akhbarana an abi sa'id al khudri radi Allahu anhu qal: qala al nabi salla Allahu alayhi wa sallam: "kaifa anam wa qad itakhadha sahib al qarn al qarn fa hwa yunfikhu fihi, qal: kaann ra'sahu kaannahu jabal". Qal: fa qalu: ya rasul Allah, fa ma ta'murana? Qal: "kunu ala basirah, wasbiru".

Abu Sa'id al-Khudri, may Allah be pleased with him, reported that the Prophet peace be upon him, said: "How can I feel at ease when the Angel of the Trumpet, (Israfil, one of the four arc angels) has put his lips to the Trumpet and is waiting for the order to blow it". He, peace be upon him, perceived as though this had shocked his companions, so he told them to seek comfort through reciting: 'Hasbunallah wa ni'mal wakeel ['Allah (Alone) is Sufficient for us, and He is the Best Disposer of affairs (for us)']".

Source: Tirmidhi, 2431

Dua for Acceptance of Fasting

اللَّهُمَّ لك صمت، وبك آمنت، وعلى رزقك أفطرت

Allahumma laka sumtu, wa bika amantu, wa 'ala rizqika aftartu

O Allah, for You have I fasted, in You do I believe, and with Your provision do I break my fast.

Source: Sunan Abi Dawood 2358.

Story of Wisdom:

أَفَلَا يَتَدَبَّرُونَ الْقُرْآنَ ۚ وَلَوْ كَانَ مِنْ عِندِ غَيْرِ
اللَّهِ لَوَجَدُوا فِيهِ اخْتِلَافًا كَثِيرًا

Afala yatadabbaroona al-Qur'ana. Walaw kana min 'indi ghayri Allahi lawajadoo feehi ikhtilafan katheera

Do they not then consider the Qur'an carefully? Had it been from other than Allah, they would surely have found therein much contradiction.

Source: Qur'an 4:82.

Dua for Performing Hajj and Umrah

اللَّهُمَّ إِنِّي أَعُوذُ بِكَ مِنْ عَذَابِ النَّارِ وَفِتْنَةِ النَّارِ ، وَفِتْنَةِ
الْغِنَى ، وَفِتْنَةِ الْفَقْرِ ، وَمِنْ شَرِّ فِتْنَةِ الْمَسِيحِ الدَّجَّالِ

Allahumma inni a'udhu bika min 'adhabi-nnar wa fitnatinnar, wa fitnatil ghina, wa fitnatil faqr, wa min sharri fitnatil masihid dajjal.

Oh Allah, I seek refuge with You from the torment of the fire and from the trials of wealth and poverty, and from the evils of the tribulations of the Antichrist.

Source: Sahih Muslim 590.

Story of Wisdom:

وَكَانَ النَّبِيُّ صَلَّى اللهُ عَلَيْهِ و سَلَّمَ يَقُولُ: إِذَا أَرَادَ اللهُ بِعَبْدِهِ
الخَيْرَ عَجَّلَ لَهُ الْعُقُوبَةَ فِي الدُّنْيَا ، وَإِذَا أَرَادَ اللهُ بِعَبْدِهِ
الشَّرَّ أَمْسَكَ عَنْهُ بِذَنْبِهِ حَتَّى يُوَافِيَ بِهِ يَوْمَ الْقِيَامَةِ

Wa kana an-nabiyyu salla Allah 'alayhi wa sallam yaqool: idha aradallahu bi 'abdihil khayra 'ajjala lahu al-'uqoobata fid-dunya, wa idha aradallahu bi 'abdihish sharra amsaka 'anhu bi dhanbihi hatta yuwaafi bihi yawma-l-qiyaamah.

The Prophet (peace be upon him) used to say: If Allah wants good for His servant, He hastens his punishment in this world, but if He wants evil for His servant, He withholds his sins from him until He gives it to him on the Day of Judgment.

Source: Jami` at-Tirmidhi 2396.

Dua for Recitation of the Qur'an

بِسْمِ اللَّهِ الرَّحْمٰنِ الرَّحِيمِ اللَّهُمَّ افْتَحْ لِي أَبْوَابَ رَحْمَتِكَ
وَارْزُقْنِي فِي الدُّنْيَا وَالْآخِرَةِ وَاجْعَلْ لِي فِي قَلْبِي فَوَ
اِسْلِ فِي وَسَمْعِي فِي بَصَرِي وَمِنْ فَوْقِي وَمِنْ تَحْتِي وَعَنْ
يَمِينِي وَعَنْ شِمَالِي وَمِنْ أَمَامِي وَمِنْ خَلْفِي وَاجْعَلْ لِي نُورًا

Bismillah ar-Rahman ar-Raheem. Allahumma aftah li abwaba rahmatika warzuqni fi ad-dunya wal akhirah. Waj'al li nooran fee qalbi wa fee lisani wa fee sam'i wa fee basari wa min fawqi wa min tahti wa an yameeni wa an shimali wa min amami wa min khalfi waj'al li noora.

In the name of Allah, the Most Gracious, the Most Merciful. Oh Allah, open the doors of Your mercy for me, and provide me sustenance in this world and the Hereafter. And place light in my heart, and on my tongue, and in my hearing, and in my sight, and above me, and below me, and on my right, and on my left, and before me, and behind me. And make for me light.

Source: Sahih Muslim

Story of Wisdom:

وَعَنِ النُّعْمَانِ بْنِ بَشِيرٍ رَضِيَ اللَّهُ عَنْهُمَا قَالَ: قَالَ رَسُولُ اللَّهِ صَلَّى
اللَّهُ عَلَيْهِ وَسَلَّمَ: مَثَلُ الْقَائِمِ عَلَى حُدُودِ اللَّهِ وَالْوَاقِعِ فِيهَا كَمَثَلِ قَوْمِ
اسْتَهَمُوا عَلَى سَفِينَةٍ فَأَصَابَ بَعْضُهُمْ أَعْلَاهَا وَبَعْضُهُمْ أَسْفَلَهَا فَكَانَ الَّذِينَ فِي أَسْفَلِهَا اِذَا اسْتَقَوْا مِنَ الْمَاءِ مَرُّوا عَلَى مَنْ فَوْقَهُمْ فَقَالُوا
لَوْ أَنَّا خَرَقْنَا فِي نَصِيبِنَا خَرْقًا وَلَمْ نُؤْذِ مَنْ فَوْقَنَا فَإِنْ يَتْرُكُوهُمْ وَمَا أَرَادُوا هَلَكُوا جَمِيعًا وَإِنْ أَخَذُوا عَلَى أَيْدِيهِمْ نَجَوْا وَنَجَوْا جَمِيعًا

Wa'an an-Nu'mani ibn Bashir radiyallahu 'anhuma qala: Qala Rasulullah sallallahu 'alayhi wa sallam: Mathalu al-qa'imi 'ala hudoodillahi wal-waqi'i feeha ka mathali qawmin istahamu 'ala safinatin fa asaba ba'duhum a'laaha wa ba'duhum asfalaha fakana alladheena fee asfaliha idha istaqaw mina al-ma'i marro 'ala man fawqahum faqalu law anna kharqna fee naseebina kharqan walam nu'dhi man fawqana fa in yatrukuhum wa ma aradu halaku jamee'an wa in akhadhu 'ala aydihim najaw wa najaw jamee'an.

From An-Nu'man ibn Bashir, may Allah be pleased with them, who said: The Messenger of Allah, peace and blessings be upon him, said: The similarity of the person abiding by Allah's orders and restrictions and the one who falls into doubtful matters is like the example of a group of people who drew lots for their places on a ship. Some of them got places in the upper part, and the others in the lower. When the latter needed water, they had to go up to bring water. They said: 'Let us make a hole in our share of the ship and get water without causing trouble to the others.' If they were let to do what they suggested all would be destroyed, but if they were stopped, all would be saved.

Source: Sahih al-Bukhari 2652

Dua for Seeking Knowledge in Religion

اللَّهُمَّ انفَعني بما عَلَّمتني و عَلِّمني ما يَنفَعني و زِدني عِلما

Allahumma anfa'ni bima 'allamtani wa 'allamni ma yanfa'ni wa zidni 'ilma

Oh Allah, benefit me from what You have taught me, and teach me what will benefit me, and increase me in knowledge.

Source: Jami` at-Tirmidhi 3599

Story of Wisdom:

وقال الرجل لابنه: يا بُنَيّ، لا تذهب بأمرك إلى من لا يُقدِرُكَ ولا يُحسِنُ ظَنَّهُ بكَ، فإنه لا يَنصح لِمن جفاهُ، ولا يُعطي لِمن لا يُحسِنُ ظَنَّهُ بالعطاء

Wa qala al-rajul li-ibnihi: Ya bunay, la tadhhab bi-amrika ila man la yuqdiruka wa la yuhsinu dhannahu bika, fa innahu la yunsih li-man jafahu, wa la yu'ti li-man la yuhsinu dhannahu bil-'ataa.

And the man said to his son, "Oh my son, do not take your affairs to someone who does not appreciate you and does not think well of you, for he will not advise someone who has treated him harshly, and he will not give to someone who does not think well of giving."

Source: Al-Adab Al-Mufrad 538 by Imam Bukhari

Dua for Protection from Shirk
(Associating Partners with Allah)

اللّهُمَّ إِنّي أَعوذ بك أن أشرك بك شيئاً وأنا أعلم، وأستغفرك لما لا أعلم

Allahumma inni a'udhu bika an ushrika bika shay'an wa ana a'lamu, wa astaghfiruka lima la a'lam.

Oh Allah, I seek refuge in You lest I associate anything with You knowingly, and I seek Your forgiveness for what I know not.

Source: Abu Dawood (Book 16, Hadith 1423)

Story of Wisdom:

قال النّبيّ محمد صلّى الله عليه وسلّم: إنّ الرجل ليتكلّم بالكلمة من رضا الله لا يلقي لها بالاً يرفع الله بها درجات، وإنّ الرجل ليتكلّم بالكلمة من سخط الله لا يلقي لها بالاً يهوي بها في جهنّم

Qala an-Nabiyy Muhammad sallallahu 'alayhi wa sallam: "Inna al-rajula layatakallamu bil-kalimati min rida Allah la yulqi laha balan yarfa'u Allahu biha darajat, wa inna al-rajula layatakallamu bil-kalimati min sakhat Allah la yulqi laha balan yahwi biha fi jahannam."

The Prophet Muhammad, peace be upon him, said: "A man speaks a word pleasing to Allah without considering it significant, but Allah exalts his rank for it. And indeed, a man speaks a word displeasing to Allah without considering it significant, but for it, he will sink down into Hell."

Source: Sahih Al-Bukhari (Book 81, Hadith 66)

Dua for Keeping up with Five Daily Prayers

اللّهُمَّ إِنّي أسألك فعل الخيرات، وترك المنكرات، وحبّ المساكين، وأن تغفر لي وترحمني، وإذا أردت فتنة قوم فتوفّني غير مفتون، وأسألك حبّك وحبّ من يحبّك وحبّ عمل يقرّبني إلى حبّك

Allahumma inni as'aluka fi'lal al-khayrat, wa tark al-munkarat, wa hubb al-masakeen, wa an taghfira li, wa tarhamni, wa idha aradta fitnatan li qawmin fatawaffani ghaira maftun, wa as'aluka hubbaka, wa hubb man yuhibbuka, wa al-'amal alladhee yuqarribuni ila hubbik

Oh Allah, I ask You to enable me to do good deeds, and to abstain from bad deeds, and to love the poor. And forgive me, and be merciful to me. And if You wish a trial for a people, then cause me to die untested. And I ask You for Your love, and the love of those who love You, and the deeds which will draw me closer to Your love.

Source: Jami` at-Tirmidhi 3235

Story of Wisdom:

عن عائشة رضي الله عنها قالت: قال رسول الله صلّى الله عليه وسلّم: ما زال جبريل يوصيني بالجار حتّى ظننت أنّه سيورثه

`An `A'ishah radi allahu `anha qalat: qala rasul Allahi salla Allah `alayhi wa sallam: ma zala Jibril yusini bil-jar hatta zhannantu annahu sayuwarithuhu.

Narrated by Aisha, may Allah be pleased with her, The Messenger of Allah, peace be upon him, said: "Gabriel continued to recommend me to treat my neighbors kindly and politely so much so that I thought he would order me to make them my heirs."

Source: Sahih al-Bukhari 6014

Dua for Parents and Ancestors

رَبِّ ارْحَمْهُمَا كَمَا رَبَّيَانِي صَغِيرًا

Rabbi irhamhuma kama rabbayani saghira

My Lord, have mercy upon them as they brought me up when I was small.

Source: Qur'an 17:24

Story of Wisdom:

قَالَ أَتَعْجَبِينَ مِنْ أَمْرِ اللَّهِ ۖ رَحْمَتُ اللَّهِ وَبَرَكَاتُهُ عَلَيْكُمْ أَهْلَ الْبَيْتِ ۚ إِنَّهُ حَمِيدٌ مَّجِيدٌ

Qala ataAAjabeena min amri Allahi rahmatu Allahi wabarakaatuhu AAalaykum ahla albayti innahu hameedun majeed

He said, "Are you astonished at the decree of Allah? May the mercy of Allah and His blessings be upon you, people of the house. Indeed, He is Praiseworthy, Glorious."

Source: Qur'an 11:73

Dua for the Deceased Muslims

اللَّهُمَّ اغفِر لَه وارحمهُ وعافِه واعفُ عنه، وأكرِم نزلَه ووسّع مدخلَه
واغسِلهُ بالماءِ والثلجِ والبردِ ونقّهِ من الخطايا كما يُنقّى الثوبُ
الأبيضُ من الدنسِ. اللَّهُمَّ أبدلهُ داراً خيرًا من دارِه وأهلاً خيرًا من
أهلِه. اللَّهُمَّ أدخلهُ الجنّةَ وأعذهُ من عذابِ القبرِ ومِن عذابِ النارِ

Allahumma-ghfir lahu warhamhu wa'afihi wa'fu 'anhu, wa akrim nuzulahu wa wassi' mudkhalahu, wagh-silhu bil-mai wath-thalji wal-baradi, wa naqqihi minal-khataaya kama yunaqqa ath-thawbul-abyadu minad-danasi. Allahumma abdilhu daaran khairan min daarihi wa ahlan khairan min ahlihi. Allahumma adkhilhul jannah wa'i'dhhu min ,adhabil-qabri wa min ,adhabin-naar.

O Allah, forgive him, have mercy on him, pardon him, grant him security, provide him a nice place and spacious lodgings, wash him (off from his sins) with water, snow and ice, purify him from his sins as a white garment is cleansed from dirt. O Allah, replace his home for a better home, and his family for a better family. O Allah, admit him to Paradise and protect him from the torment of the grave and from the torment of fire.

Source: Sahih Muslim 924

Story of Wisdom:

وَإِذْ أَخَذَ اللَّهُ مِيثَاقَ الَّذِينَ أُوتُوا الْكِتَابَ لَتُبَيِّنُنَّهُ لِلنَّاسِ وَلَا تَكْتُمُونَهُ فَنَبَذُوهُ وَرَاءَ ظُهُورِهِمْ وَاشْتَرَوْا بِهِ ثَمَنًا قَلِيلًا فَبِئْسَ مَا يَشْتَرُونَ

Akhadha Allahu meethaqa allatheena ootoo alkitaba latubayyinunnahu lilnnasi wala taktumoonahu fanabathoohu waraa thuhoorihim wa ishtaraw bihi thamanan qaleelan fabi'sa ma yashtaroon

Allah has taken a promise from those who were given the Book (Jews and Christians): 'You will make it known clearly to mankind and not hide it.' But they threw it away behind their backs and purchased with it some petty gain. What an evil trade they made!

Source: Qur'an 3:187

Dua for Avoiding Major Sins

اللَّهُمَّ إِنِّي أَعُوذُ بِكَ مِنَ الْمَأْثَمِ وَالْمَغْرَمِ

Allahumma inni a'udhu bika minal-ma'thami wal-maghrami

Oh Allah, I seek refuge with You from sinning and being in debt.

Source: Sahih al-Bukhari 832

Story of Wisdom:

وَقُل رَّبِّ أَعُوذُ بِكَ مِنْ هَمَزَاتِ الشَّيَاطِينِ

وَأَعُوذُ بِكَ رَبِّ أَن يَحْضُرُونِ

Wa qul rabbi a'udhu bika min hamazati al-shayatin, Wa a'udhu bika rabbi an yahdurun

And say, 'My Lord, I seek refuge with You from the incitements of the devils, and I seek refuge with You, my Lord, lest they be present with me.'"

Source: Holy Qur'an, Surah Al-Mu'minun (23:97-98)

Dua for Preparing for Death and the Hereafter

اللَّهُمَّ إِنِّي أَعُوذُ بِكَ مِنْ فِتْنَةِ الْمَسِيحِ الدَّجَّالِ، وَأَعُوذُ بِكَ مِنْ عَذَابِ الْقَبْرِ، وَأَعُوذُ بِكَ مِنْ فِتْنَةِ الْمَحْيَا وَالْمَمَاتِ. اللَّهُمَّ إِنِّي أَعُوذُ بِكَ مِنَ الْمَأْثَمِ وَالْمَغْرَمِ

Allahumma inni a'udhu bika min 'adhabil-qabr, wa a'udhu bika min fitnatil-masihi d-dajjal, wa a'udhu bika min fitnatil-mahya wal-mamat. Allahumma inni a'udhu bika minal-ma'thami wal-maghram

Oh Allah, I seek refuge with You from the punishment of the grave and the trials of the False Messiah, and I seek refuge in You from the trials of life and death. Oh Allah, I seek refuge with You from sins and from being in debt.

Source: Sahih Bukhari 832

Story of Wisdom:

عَنْ أَبِى هُرَيْرَةَ قَالَ قَالَ رَسُولُ اللَّهِ صَلَّى اللهُ عَلَيهِ وسَلَّمَ مَنْ
قَالَ لَا إِلَهَ إِالَّا اللَّهُ وَفَىَ بِهَا مُتَّى وَهُوَ يَحْتَدِى بِهَا دَخَلَ الْجَنَّةَ

An abi Hurayra qaal qaala rasoolul-lahi sallallahu alayhi wa sallam man qaal
laa ilaha illaa Allah wa faa bihaa mutta wa huwa yahtadi bihaa dakhala al-
Jannah

Narrated Abu Huraira: The Messenger of Allah said, "Whoever says there is
no god but Allah and dies while adhering to that will enter Paradise."

Source: Sahih Bukhari 5831

Chapter 10:
Expressions of Praise: Deepening Connection with Allah

Dua for Thanking Allah for His Blessings

اللَّهُمَّ لَكَ الْحَمْدُ كُلَّهُ، وَلَكَ الْمُلْكُ كُلَّهُ، لَا إِلَهَ غَيْرُكَ،
أَعُوذُ بِكَ مِنْ شَرِّ نَفْسِي وَمِنْ شَرِّ الشَّيْطَانِ وَشِرْكِهِ، وَأَنْ
أَقْتَرِفَ عَلَى نَفْسِي سُوءًا أَوْ أَجُرَّهُ إِلَى مُسْلِمٍ

Allahumma laka al-hamdu kulluhu, wa laka al-mulku kulluhu, la ilaha ghayruka. A'udhu bika min sharri nafsi wa min sharri ash-shaytani wa shirkihi, wa an aqtarifa 'ala nafsi su'an aw ajurrahu ila muslimin.

O Allah, all praise is due to You, to You belongs all that is in the heavens and the earth. There is no diety but You. I seek refuge with You from the evil of myself, from the evil of Satan and his polytheism, and from committing wrong against myself or bringing such upon another Muslim.

Source: Sahih Muslim 2713.

Story of Wisdom:

قَالَ النَّبِيُّ صَلَّى اللهُ عَلَيْهِ وَسَلَّمَ "إِنَّ اللَّهَ كَتَبَ الْحَسَنَاتِ
وَالسَّيِّئَاتِ، ثُمَّ بَيَّنَ ذَلِكَ، فَمَنْ هَمَّ بِحَسَنَةٍ فَلَمْ يَعْمَلْهَا كَتَبَهَا اللَّهُ عِنْدَهُ
حَسَنَةً كَامِلَةً، وَإِنْ هُوَ هَمَّ بِهَا فَعَمِلَهَا كَتَبَهَا اللَّهُ عِنْدَهُ عَشْرَ حَسَنَاتٍ إِلَى
سَبْعِ مِائَةِ ضِعْفٍ إِلَى أَضْعَافٍ كَثِيرَةٍ. وَإِنْ هَمَّ بِسَيِّئَةٍ فَلَمْ يَعْمَلْهَا كَتَبَهَا
اللَّهُ عِنْدَهُ حَسَنَةً كَامِلَةً، وَإِنْ هُوَ هَمَّ بِهَا فَعَمِلَهَا كَتَبَهَا اللَّهُ سَيِّئَةً وَاحِدَةً."

Qala an-Nabiyyu salla Allahu 'alayhi wa sallam "Inna Allaha kataba al-hasanati wa al-sayyi'ati, thumma bayyana thalik, faman hamma bihasanatin falam ya'malha katabaha Allahu 'indahu hasanatan kamilatan, wa in huwa hamma biha fa'amalaha katabaha Allahu 'indahu 'ashra hasanatin ila sab'i mi'ati d'ifin ila ad'afin kathirah. wa in hamma bisayyiatin falam ya'malha katabaha Allahu 'indahu hasanatan kamilatan, wa in huwa hamma biha fa'amalaha katabaha Allahu sayyi'atan wahidatan."

The Prophet, peace be upon him, said, "Indeed, Allah has recorded the good deeds and the evil deeds, then explained that. Whoever intended to perform a good deed, but did not do it, then Allah writes it down with Himself as a complete good deed. And if he intended to perform it and did perform it, then Allah writes it down with Himself as from ten good deeds up to seven hundred fold, up to many times multiplied. If he intended to perform an evil deed, but did not do it, then Allah writes it down with Himself as a complete good deed. If he intended it [an evil deed] and then performed it, then Allah writes it down as one evil deed."

Source: Sahih al-Bukhari 6126.

Dua for Seeking Allah's Pleasure

اللّهَمَّ إنِّي أسألك رضاك والجنّة، وأعوذ بك من سخطك والنار.

Allahumma inni as'aluka ridaka wal-jannah, wa a'udhu bika min sakhtika wan-nar.

O Allah, I ask You for Your Pleasure and Paradise, and I seek refuge in You from Your Anger and the Fire.

Source: Jami` at-Tirmidhi 2581

Story of Wisdom:

قال رسول الله صلّى الله عليه وسلّم: ال يؤمن
أحدكم حتّى يحبّ لأخيه ما يحبّ لنفسه

Qala rasool Allah salla Allah alaihi wa sallam: La yu'min ahadukum hatta yuhibba li'akhihi ma yuhibbu li nafsihi.

The Messenger of Allah, peace and blessings be upon him, said: None of you truly believes until he loves for his brother what he loves for himself.

Source: Sahih al-Bukhari 13

Dua for Trust and Reliance on Allah

اللّهَمَّ إنِّي أعوذ بك أن أشرك بك وأنا أعلَمُ، وأستغفِرُك لِما ال أعلَمُ

Allahumma inni a'udhu bika an ushrika bika wa ana a'lamu, wa astaghfiruka lima la a'lam.

Oh Allah, I seek refuge in You lest I associate anything with You knowingly, and I seek Your forgiveness for what I know not.

Source: Sahih al-Bukhari 6307

Story of Wisdom:

قال النبي صلّى الله عليه وسلّم توكّلوا على الله ولكن اعقلوا وقال رجل يا رسول الله أعقلها وأتوكّل أو أتركها وأتوكّل قال لا بل اعقلها وتوكّل شهد بذلك عمرو بن العاص

Qala an-Nabi salla Allahu 'alayhi wa sallam: "Tawakkalu 'ala Allah walakin i'qilu". Wa qala rajul: Ya Rasulallah! A'qilha wa atawakkal aw atrukha wa atawakkal? Qala: "La, bal i'qilha wa tawakkal". Shahida bi dhalika 'Amru ibn al-'Aas.

The Prophet (peace be upon him) said: "Rely on Allah, but tie your camel." A man asked, "O Messenger of Allah! Should I tie my camel and trust in Allah, or should I let her loose and trust in Allah?" He said, "No, tie her and trust in Allah." Amr bin Al-Aas witnessed this.

Source: Sunan At-Tirmidhi 2517

Dua for Allah's Guidance and Light

اللّهُمّ اهْدِني فيمَنْ هَدَيْتَ، وَعافِني فيمَنْ عافَيْتَ، وَتَوَلَّني فيمَنْ تَوَلَّيْتَ، وَبارِكْ لي فيما أعْطَيْتَ، وَقِني شَرّ ما قَضَيْتَ، فَإنّكَ تَقْضي وَلا يُقْضى عَلَيْكَ، إنّهُ لا يَذِلُّ مَنْ والَيْتَ، وَلا يَعِزُّ مَنْ عادَيْتَ، تَبارَكْتَ رَبّنا وَتَعالَيْتَ

Allahumma ah-dini fiman hadayt, wa 'aafini fiman 'afayt. Wa tawallani fiman tawallayt. Wa baarik li fima a'tayt, wa qini sharra ma qadayt. Fa innaka taqdi wa la yuqda 'alayk. Innahu la yadhil-lu man walayt. Wa la ya'izzu man 'adayt. Tabarakta Rabbana wa ta'alayt.

O Allah, guide me along with those whom You have guided, pardon me along with those whom You have pardoned, be an ally to me along with those whom You are an ally to, and bless for me that which You have bestowed. Protect me from the evil You have decreed, for verily You decree and none can decree over You. Surely, he whom You ally will never be disgraced and he whom You oppose will never be honored. Blessed are You, our Lord and exalted.

Source: Sahih Muslim 2736

Story of Wisdom:

عن أبي عبد الله عبد الرحمن بن عبد الله بن مسعود رضي الله عنهما، قال: حدثنا
رسول الله صلى الله عليه وسلم وهو الصادق المصدوق: ,, إن أحدكم
يجمع خلقه في بطن أمه أربعين يوماً نطفة، ثم يكون علقة مثل ذلك،
ثم يكون مضغة مثل ذلك، ثم يرسل إليه الملك، فينفخ فيه الروح،
ويؤمر بأربع كلمات: بكتب رزقه، وأجله، وعمله، وشقي أو سعيد.

An Abi 'Abd al-Rahman 'Abd Allah ibn Mas'ud radi Allah 'anhu, qal:
Hadathna Rasul Allah salla Allah 'alayh wa sallam wa huwa al-sadiq al-
masduq: "Inna ahadakum yajma' khalaqah fi batni ummihi arba'in yawman
nutfa, thumma yakun 'alaqah mithli dhalik, thumma yakun mudghah mithli
dhalik, thumma yursil ilayh al-malak, fayunfakh fihi al-ruh, wa yu'mar bi arba'
kalimat: bi kitab rizqihi, wa ajalihi, wa 'amalihi, wa shaqi aw sa'id."

Abu 'Abd al-Rahman 'Abd Allah ibn Mas'ud, may Allah be pleased with him,
reported: The Messenger of Allah, peace and blessings be upon him, who is
truthful and verified, has informed us: "Indeed, one of you is gathered in his
mother's womb for forty days as a sperm-drop, then a clot for a period similar,
then a morsel of flesh for a similar period. Then the angel is sent to him and
breathes the soul into him. He is ordered with four words: to write down
his sustenance, his lifespan, his deeds, and whether he will be wretched or
blessed."

Source: Sahih al-Bukhari 3208, Sahih Muslim 2643

Dua for Awe of Allah's Creation

رَبَّنَا مَا خَلَقْتَ هَذَا بَاطِلاً سُبْحَانَكَ فَقِنَا عَذَابَ النَّارِ

Subhanaka ma khalaqta hadha batila, Subhanaka faqina 'adhaban-nar

Glory be to You, You did not create this in vain; glory be to You, save us from
the torment of the Fire.

Source: Surah Al-Imran (3:191)

Story of Wisdom:

قَالَتْ نَمْلَةٌ يٰأَيُّهَا النَّمْلُ ادْخُلُوا مَسَاكِنَكُمْ لَا يَحْطِمَنَّكُمْ سُلَيْمٰنُ
وَجُنُودُهُ وَهُمْ لَا يَشْعُرُونَ فَتَبَسَّمَ ضَاحِكًا مِّنْ قَوْلِهَا وَقَالَ رَبِّ أَوْزِعْنِي
أَنْ أَشْكُرَ نِعْمَتَكَ الَّتِي أَنْعَمْتَ عَلَيَّ وَعَلَىٰ وَالِدَيَّ وَأَنْ أَعْمَلَ
صَالِحًا تَرْضَاهُ وَأَدْخِلْنِي بِرَحْمَتِكَ فِي عِبَادِكَ الصَّالِحِينَ.

Qalat namlatun ya ayyuha an-namlu adkhulu masakinakum la
yahtimannakum Sulaymanu wa junooduhu wa hum la yash'urun.
Fatabassama dahikan min qawliha wa qala rabbi awzi'ni an ashkura ni'mataka
allatee an'amta 'alayya wa 'ala walidayya wa an a'mala salihan tardahu wa
adkhilni bi rahmatika fee 'ibadika as-salihin.

An ant said: "O ants, enter your dwellings that you not be crushed by
Solomon and his soldiers while they perceive not." So [Solomon] smiled,
amused at her speech, and said: "My Lord, enable me to be grateful for Your
favor which You have bestowed upon me and upon my parents and to do
righteousness of which You approve. And admit me by Your mercy into [the
ranks of] Your righteous servants."

Source: Surah An-Naml (27:18-19)

Dua for Allah's Forgiveness and Mercy

اللّٰهُمَّ إِنَّكَ عَفُوٌّ تُحِبُّ الْعَفْوَ فَاعْفُ عَنِّي

Allahumma innaka 'afuwwun, tuhibbul-'afwa, fa'fu 'anni

Oh Allah, You are Forgiving and love forgiveness, so forgive me.

Source: Sunan Ibn Majah 3828

Story of Wisdom:

قَالَ النَّبِيُّ صَلَّى اللّٰهُ عَلَيْهِ وَسلَّمَ: مَنْ قَالَ حِينَ يُصْبِحُ وَحِينَ
يُمْسِي: سُبْحَانَ اللّٰهِ وَبِحَمْدِهِ مِائَةَ مَرَّةٍ لَمْ يَأْتِ أَحَدٌ يَوْمَ الْقِيَامَةِ
بِأَفْضَلَ مَا جَاءَ بِهِ إِلَّا أَحَدٌ قَالَ مِثْلَ مَا قَالَ، أَوْ زَادَ عَلَيْهِ

Qala an-nabiyyu sallallahu 'alayhi wa sallam: man qala hina yusbihu wa hina
yumsi: subhanallahi wa bihamdihi mi'ata marra lam ya'ti ahadun yawmal
qiyamati bi afdala ma ja'a bihi illa ahadun qala mithla ma qal, aw zada 'alayhi

The Prophet, peace be upon him, said: Whoever says when he wakes up and when he goes to sleep: 'Glory be to Allah, and His is the praise', a hundred times, no one will come on the Day of Resurrection with better than what he came with, except for someone who said the same as he said, or more than that.

Source: Sahih Muslim 2692.

Dua for Steadfastness in Faith

اللّٰهُمَّ يا مقلّبَ القلوبِ والأبصارِ ثبّتْ قلبي على دينكَ

Allahumma Ya Muqallibal Quloob wal Absaar, Thabbit Qalbi 'ala Deenik

Oh Allah, The Turner of Hearts and Sight, make my heart firm upon Your religion.

Source: Sunan At-Tirmidhi 2140

Story of Wisdom:

حديث الصحيحين: قال النبيّ صلى الله عليه وسلم:
إنّ الإيمان ليخلق في قلب أحدكم كما يخلق الثوب
الخلق، فسلوا الله أن يجدّد الإيمان في قلوبكم

Hadith As-Sahihayn: Qala An-Nabiyy Sallallahu 'Alayhi wa Sallam: Inna Al-Imaan La Yakhlaqu fi Jawfi Ahadikum Kama Yakhlaq Ath-Thawb Al-Khalaq, Fas'alu Allah An Yujaddid Al-Imaan fi Quloobikum

The Prophet said, "Verily faith wears out in the heart of any one of you just as clothes wear out, so ask Allah to renew the faith in your hearts."

Source: Sahih Muslim 158.

Dua for Protection from Deviation

اللّٰهُمَّ إنِّي أعوذ بك أن أضلّ، أو أُضلَّ، أو أزلّ، أو أُزلَّ،
أو أظلِمَ، أو أُظلَمَ، أو أجهَلَ، أو يُجهَلَ عليّ.

Allahumma inni a'udhu bika an adilla, aw udalla, aw azilla, aw uzalla, aw azlima, aw uzlama, aw ajhala, aw yujhala 'alayya.

Oh Allah, I seek refuge in You that I err, go astray, stumble, am mistreated, oppress, become ignorant or be oppressed.

Source: Sahih Muslim 2708

Story of Wisdom:

عن أبي هريرة، قال: قال رسول الله صلّى الله عليه وسلّم: ,,اذا دعا الإنسان بدعوة ليس فيها إثم ولا قطيعة رحم، اعطاه الله لها بها أحد ثلاث: إما أن يجعل له دعوته، واما أن يدخر هرا له في الآخرة، واما أن يصرف عنه من السوء مثلها. قالوا: فنكثر. قال: الله أكثر.‟

An abi hurayra, qal: qal rasul allah salla allah alayh wa sallam: "Idha da'a al-insaanu bida'watin laysa fiha ithmun wala qati'atu rahmin, i'tadala Allah lahu biha ahd thalathah: ima an yu'jila lahu da'watuhu, wa ima an yadakhiraha lahu fil-akhirati, wa ima an yasrifa 'anhu min as-su'i mithlaha. qalu: fa nukthir. qal: Allahu akthar."

Narrated on the authority of Abu Huraira that the Messenger of Allah said: "When a person supplicates and his supplication does not contain sin or cutting of relations, Allah fulfills one of three things: He may speedily answer his supplication, or He may store it up for him in the Hereafter, or He may divert an equivalent evil away from him". They said: Should we then be plentiful in supplication? He said: Allah is more plentiful (in responding).

Source: Sahih Muslim 2736

Dua for Sincerity in Worship

اللّهُمَّ إِنِّي أَعُـوذُ بِكَ أَنْ أُشْرِكَ بِكَ وَأَنَا أَعْلَمُ، وَأَسْتَغْفِرُكَ لِمَا لَا أَعْلَمُ

Allahumma inni a'udhu bika an ushrika bika wa ana a'lamu, wa astaghfiruka li ma la a'lamu

Oh Allah, I seek refuge in You from associating anything with You knowingly, and I seek Your forgiveness for that which I do unknowingly.

Source: At-Tirmidhi 3533

Story of Wisdom:

قَالَ الَّنبِي صَلَّى اللَّه عليه وَسَلَّمْ ٱٱ الدِّينُ النَّصِيحَةُ قُلْنَا لِمَنْ
قَالَ لِلَّلِ وَلِكِتَابِهِ وَلِرَسُولِهِ وَلِأَئِمَّةِ الْمُسْلِمِينَ وَعَامَّتِهِمْٱٱ

Qal an-nabiyu salla Allahu alaihi wasallam "ad-deenu an-naseeha" qulna liman? Qala: lillahi wa li kitabihi wa li rasoolihi wa li a'immati al-muslimeen wa 'ammatihim

The Prophet, peace be upon him, said: "Religion is sincerity." We asked: "To whom?" He replied: "To Allah, His Book, His Messenger, and to the leaders of the Muslims and their common folk."

Source: Sahih Muslim 55

Dua for Acknowledging Allah's Majesty

سبحانك اللَّهمَّ وبحمدك، وتبارك اسمك، وتعالى جدّك، ولا إله غيرك

Subhanaka Allahumma wa bihamdika, wa tabarakasmuka, wa ta'ala jadduka, wa la ilaha ghairuk.

Glory be to You, O Allah, and all praises are due unto You, and blessed is Your name and high is Your majesty and none is worthy of worship but You.

Source: At-Tirmidhi 3451

Story of Wisdom:

قال الَّنبيّ صلَّى اللَّه عليه وسلَّم: ,,الدُّنيا ملعونة
ملعون ما فيها إلا ذكر اللَّه وما والاه وعالم أو متعلم"

Qala an-Nabiyy sallallahu 'alaihi wasallam: "Ad-dunya mal'oonah. Mal'oonun maa feeha illa dhikrullahi wa maa waalah wa 'aalimun aw muta'allimun."

The Prophet peace be upon him said: "The world is cursed. Cursed is what is in it except for the remembrance of Allah, what is related to it, a knowledgeable person or one who is learning."

Source: At-Tirmidhi 2322

Dua for Hope in Allah's Compassion

رّ يقِفَ رٍ يْخَ نْ مّ يلَ إِ تلْزَنأ امَلِ ينّ إِ بَرَ

Rabbi inni lima anzalta ilayya min khairin faqeer

O my Lord, I am in absolute need of the good You send me.

Source: Quran 28:24

Story of Wisdom:

ابَّقُحُ يَضِمْأ وْ أِ نيْرَ حْبَلْاَ عمَجُمَ غلُبْأ ىتَّحَ حُرَبْأ الَ ُهاتَفَلِ ىسَومُ لَ اقَ ذْإِ و

Wa iz qaala Moosa liFataahu laa abrahu hatta ablugha majma' al-bahrayn aw amdiya huquba.

And (remember) when Moses said to his servant: "I will not give up until I reach the junction of the two seas or (until) I spend years and years in travel."

Source: Quran 18:60

Chapter 11:
Relationship Harmony: Duas
for Interpersonal Bonds

Dua for Respectful and Loving Relationships

رَبَّنَا هَبْ لَنَا مِنْ أَزْوَاجِنَا وَذُرِّيَّاتِنَا قُرَّةَ أَعْيُنٍ وَاجْعَلْنَا لِلْمُتَّقِينَ إِمَامًا

Rabbana hab lana min azwajina wa dhurriyatina qurrata a'yuni wa-j'alna lil-muttaqina imama

Our Lord, grant us from among our wives and offspring comfort to our eyes and make us an example for the righteous.

Source: Quran, 25:74

Story of Wisdom:

قَالَ رَسُولُ اللهِ صَلَّى اللهُ عَلَيْهِ وَسَلَّمَ ، إِنَّ "خَيْرُكُمْ
خَيْرُكُمْ لِأَهْلِهِ وَأَنَا خَيْرُكُمْ لِأَهْلِي

Qala rasoolu allahi salla Allahu alayhe wa sallam "khayrukum khayrukum li'ahlihi wa ana khayrukum li'ahli"

The Prophet Muhammad (peace be upon him) said: "The best of you is the best to his family, and I am the best among you to my family".

Source: Tirmidhi, Hadith 3895.

Dua for Reconciliation and Peace

اللَّهُمَّ أَصْلِحْ لِي دِينِي الَّذِي هُوَ عِصْمَةُ أَمْرِي ، وَأَصْلِحْ لِي دُنْيَايَ الَّتِي فِيهَا مَعَاشِي ، وَأَصْلِحْ لِي آخِرَتِي الَّتِي فِيهَا مَعَادِي ، وَاجْعَلِ الْحَيَاةَ زِيَادَةً لِي فِي كُلِّ خَيْرٍ ، وَاجْعَلِ الْمَوْتَ رَاحَةً لِي مِنْ كُلِّ شَرٍّ

Allahumma aslih li deeni alladhee huwa 'ismatu amri, wa aslih li dunyaaya allatee feehaa ma'aashee, wa aslih li aakhiratee allatee feehaa ma'aadee, waj'alil-hayaata ziyaadatan li fee kulli khayr, waj'alil-mawta raahatan li min kulli sharr.

Oh Allah, correct for me my religion which is my safeguard, and correct for me my world where my livelihood lies, and correct for me my Hereafter to which is my return, and make life an increase for me in every good, and make death a rest for me from every evil.

Source: Sahih Muslim 2720

Story of Wisdom:

قَالَ النَّبِيُّ صَلَّى اللهُ عَلَيهِ وسَلَّمَ ﴿لَا تَحَاسَدُوا،
وَلَا تَنَاجَشُوا، وَلَا تَبَاغَضُوا، وَلَا تَدَابَرُوا، وَلَا يَبِعْ
بَعْضُكُمْ عَلَى بَيْعِ بَعْضٍ؛ وَكُونُوا عِبَادَ اللَّهِ إِخْوَانًا

Qala al-nabiyyu salla Allahu alaihi wa-sallam "la tahasadu, wa la tanajashu, wa la tabaghadu, wa la tadabaru, wa la yabi' ba'adukum 'ala bay'i ba'ad, wa kunu 'ibad Allah ikhwanan."

The Prophet (peace and blessings be upon him) said, "Do not envy one another, do not inflate prices by overbidding against one another, do not hate one another, do not turn away from one another, and do not undercut one another in trade, but be you, O servants of Allah, brothers.

Source: Sahih Muslim 2564.

Dua for Good Relations with Neighbors

اللَّهُمَّ اجعَلنِي خَيرًا مِمَّا يَظُنُّونَ، واغفِر لِي مَا لَا
يَعلَمُونَ، وَلَا تُؤاخِذنِي بِمَا يَقُولُونَ

Allahumma ij'alni khayran mimma yadhunoon, wa ghfir li ma la ya'lamoon, wa la tu'akhithni bima yaqooloon

Oh Allah, make me better than what they think, forgive me for what they do not know, and do not take me to account for what they say.

Source: Jami` at-Tirmidhi 3545

Story of Wisdom:

عن أنس بن مالك رضي الله عنه أن النبيّ صلّى الله عليه و
سلّم قال: الي يؤمن أحدكم حتّى يحبّ لأخيه ما يحبّ لنفسه"

'An Anas bin Malik radi Allahu 'anhu annan Nabi salla Allah 'alayh wa sallam qal: "La yu'min ahadukum hatta yuhibba li'akhihi ma yuhibbu linafsihi"

Narrated Anas bin Malik: The Prophet (peace be upon him) said, "None of you will have faith till he loves for his brother what he loves for himself."

Source: Sahih al-Bukhari 13

Dua for Kindness Towards Parents

رَبِّ ارْحَمْهُمَا كَمَا رَبَّيَانِي صَغِيرًا

Rabbi irhamhuma kama rabbayani saghira

Oh Lord! Show mercy on them, as they nurtured me when I was young.

Source: Quran 17:24

Story of Wisdom:

قَالَ لَهُ صَاحِبُهُ وَهُوَ يُحَاوِرُهُ أَكَفَرْتَ بِالَّذِي خَلَقَكَ
مِن تُرَابٍ ثُمَّ مِن نُّطْفَةٍ ثُمَّ سَوَّاكَ رَجُلًا

Qala lahu sahibuhu wahuwa yuhawiruhu akafarta billadhee khalaqaka min turabin thumma min nutfatin thumma sawwaka rajula

His friend said to him while he was conversing with him, "Do you deny the One who created you from dust, then from a sperm-drop, then shaped you into a man?

Source: Quran 18:37

Dua for Righteous Offspring

رَبِّ هَبْ لِي مِن لَّدُنكَ ذُرِّيَّةً طَيِّبَةً ۖ إِنَّكَ سَمِيعُ الدُّعَاءِ

Rabbi hab li min ladunka dhurriyyatan tayyibatan. Innaka Samee'ud-Dua'a

O my Lord, grant me from Yourself a good offspring. Indeed, You are the Hearer of supplication.

Source: Quran, 3:38

Story of Wisdom:

يتِأَرَمْا تِنَاكَوَ مْالَغُ يِلِ نْوكُيَ ىٰنَأَ ِبِرَ لَاقَ
ايِّتِعِ رِبَكِلْا نَمِ تْغْلَبَ دْقَوَ ارِقاعَ

Qala rabbi anna yakoonu li ghulamun wakanati imraati 'aqiran waqad balaghtu mina alkibari 'itiyya

He said, "My Lord, how will I have a boy when my wife has been barren and I have reached extreme old age?"

Source: Quran, 19:8

Dua for Blessings in Marriage

رِ انَّلا بِاذَعَ انَقِوَ انَتَقْزَرَ امَيِف انَلَ كْرِاب مَّهْللا

Allahumma barik lana fima razaqtana wa qina 'adhaban-nar

O Allah, bless for us what You have provided us and protect us from the punishment of the Fire.

Source: Sahih al-Bukhari 3343

Story of Wisdom:

مْكُرِيْخَ ["]مْلّسَو هيِلعَ اللها ىلّصَ هلَّلْا لْوسُرَ لَاقَ
يلِهْأَل مْكُرِيْخَ انَاَوَ هِلِهْأَل مْكُرِيْخَ

Qala rasulu llahi salla llahu 'alay-hi wa-sallam "khayrukum khayrukum li'ahlih, wa ana khayrukum li'ahli"

The Messenger of Allah said, "The best of you is the best to his family, and I am the best among you to my family."

Source: Jami` at-Tirmidhi 3895

Dua for Brotherhood in Faith

اللَّهُمَّ اجْعَلْنَا وَإِيَّاكُمْ مِنْ أَهْلِ الْفِرْدَوْسِ الأَعْلَى مَعَ
النَّبِيِّينَ وَالصِّدِّيقِينَ وَالشُّهَدَاءِ وَالصَّالِحِينَ

Allahumma aj'alna wa iyyakum min Ahli al-Firdaws al-A'la ma'an-Nabiyin was-Siddiqin wash-Shuhada' was-Salihin

O Allah, make us and you among the people of the highest Paradise with the Prophets, the truthful, the martyrs, and the righteous.

Source: Jami` at-Tirmidhi 3501

Story of Wisdom:

وَأَقْسَمُوا بِاللَّهِ جَهْدَ أَيْمَانِهِمْ لَا يَبْعَثُ اللَّهُ مَن يَمُوتُ بَلَىٰ
وَعْدًا عَلَيْهِ حَقًّا وَلَٰكِنَّ أَكْثَرَ النَّاسِ لَا يَعْلَمُونَ

Wa aqsamoo billahi jahda aymanihim la yab'athu Allah man yamoot. Bala wa'dan 'alayhi haqqañ, walakinna aktharan nasi la ya'lamoon.

And they swear by Allah their strongest oaths that Allah will not resurrect one who dies. But yes – it is a promise binding upon Him, but most of the people do not know.

Source: Surah An-Nahl (16:38)

Dua for Protecting Friendships

اللَّهُمَّ اجعل انا أصدقاء لَلَّذِينَ يؤمنون وأعداءَ لَلَّذِينَ يكفرون

Allahumma ija'alna asdiqa' lilladheena yu'minoon wa 'adaa' lilladheena yakfuroon

O Allah, make us friends of the believers and enemies of the disbelievers.

Source: General Dua

Story of Wisdom:

قال رسول الله صلّى الله عليه وسلّم: "المرء على
دين خليله، فلينظر أحدكم من يخالل"،

Qala rasool Allahi salla Allahu 'alayhi wa sallam: "Almar'u 'ala deen khalilihi, falyanzur ahadukum man yukhalil"

The Prophet Muhammad (peace be upon him) said: "A person follows the religion of his close friend; therefore, let each of you look carefully at whom he befriends."

Source: Sunan Abi Dawood 4833

Dua for Empathy and Understanding

اللّهمّ ارزقنا فهم الناس كما يريدون أن يفهمونا

Allahumma arzuqna fahman-nas kama yuridoona an yafhamoona

O Allah, grant us the ability to understand others as they wish to be understood.

Source: Hadith Qudsi 18

Story of Wisdom:

قال النبيّ محمّد صلّى الله عليه وسلّم): ال يؤمن
أحدكم حتّى يحبّ لأخيه ما يحبّ لنفسه)

Qaal an-nabi Muhammad (salla Allah 'alayh wa sallam): "La yu'min ahadukum hatta yuhibba li'akhihi ma yuhibbu linafsihi"

Prophet Muhammad (peace be upon him) said: "None of you truly believes until he loves for his brother what he loves for himself".

Source: Sahih al-Bukhari 13

Dua for Support During Family Trials

اللّهمّ إنّي أسألك الهدى والتقى والعفاف والغنى

Allahumma inni as'aluka al-huda wa't-tuqa wa'l-'afafa wa'l-ghina

Oh Allah, I ask You for guidance, piety, chastity, and contentment.

Source: Sahih Muslim 2721

Story of Wisdom:

قالَ النّبيِّ محمد صلّى الله عليه وسلّم: إنّما بُعِثْتُ لأُتمِّمَ مَكارِمَ الأَخْلَاقِ

Qala an-nabi Muhammad sallallahu alayhi wasallam: innama bu'ithtu li-utammima makarima al-akhlaq

The Prophet Muhammad (peace be upon him) said: I have been sent to perfect good character.

Source: Al-Muwatta 1614

Dua for Guidance for Children

اللّهَمَّ اجعلني من الّذين يستمعون القول فيتّبعون أحسنه

Allahumma ijalni minalladhina yastami'una alqawla fayattabi'una ahsanahu

Oh Allah, make me among those who listen to the word and follow the best of it.

Source: Quran 39:18

Story of Wisdom:

قال رسول الله صلّى الله عليه وسلّم: أفضلكم من تعلّم القرآن وعلمه

Qala rasulullah sallallahu alayhi wasallam: Afdalukum man ta'allama al-Quran wa'allamah

The Messenger of Allah (peace be upon him) said: The best among you are those who learn the Quran and teach it.

Source: Sahih al-Bukhari 5027

Dua for Unity in the Ummah

اللّهُمَّ اجعلنا جميعاً مِن أُمَّةِ محمَّد صلَّى اللّه علَيهِ وسلّم
واجعلنا يداً واحدةً ولا تجعل بيننا الفتنتن ولا النزاع

Allahumma ij'alna jamee'an min ummati Muhammad salla Allahu 'alayhi wa sallam wa ij'alna yadan wahidatan wa la taj'al baynana al-fitna wa la al-nizaa'

O Allah, make us all from the nation of Muhammad, may Allah bless him and grant him peace, and make us one hand, and do not cause dissension and dispute among us.

Source: Dua from Hadith

Story of Wisdom:

قال رسول اللّه صلَّى اللّه علَيهِ وسلّم: ,,لا تباغضوا،
ولا تحاسدوا، ولا تدابروا، وكونوا عباد اللّه إخواناً''

Qala rasul Allahi salla Allahu 'alayhi wa sallam: "La tabaghadu, wa la tahasadu, wa la tadabaru, wa kunu 'ibad Allahi ikhwana."

The Messenger of Allah, may Allah bless him and grant him peace, said, "Do not envy one another, do not hate one another, do not turn away from one another, but rather be servants of Allah as brothers."

Source: Sahih Muslim, Book 32, Hadith 6219

Dua for Compassion Among Believers

اللّهُمَّ ارزقنا حبَّك وحبَّ من يحبّك وحبَّ كل عمل يقرّبنا إلى حبَّك

Allahumma arzuqna hubbak wa hubba man yuhibbuk wa hubba kulli 'amalin yuqarribuna ila hubbik

Oh Allah, grant us Your love, the love of those who love You, and the love of deeds that bring us closer to Your love.

Source: Tirmidhi 3490

Story of Wisdom:

قال رسول الله صلّى الله عليه وسلّم: "لا يؤمن
أحدكم حتّى يحبّ لأخيه ما يحبّ لنفسه"

Qala rasoolullahi salla Allahu 'alayhi wa sallam: "La yuminu ahadukum hatta yuhibba li akhihi ma yuhibbu li nafsihi."

The Messenger of Allah, peace and blessings be upon him, said, "None of you truly believes until he loves for his brother what he loves for himself."

Source: Sahih Bukhari 13

Dua for Forgiveness Between Muslims

رَبَّنَا فَاغْفِرْ لَنَا ذُنُوبَنَا وَكَفِّرْ عَنَّا سَيِّئَاتِنَا وَتَوَفَّنَا مَعَ الْأَبْرَارِ

Rabbana faghfir lana dhunoobana wa kaffir 'ana sayyi'aatina wa tawaffana ma'al abrar

Our Lord, so forgive us our sins and remove from us our misdeeds and cause us to die with the righteous.

Source: Holy Quran, Surah Al-Imran (3:193)

Story of Wisdom:

عن عبد الله بن عمر أنّ رسول الله صلّى الله عليه وسلّم قال: ما من
مسلم يغفر لمسلم إلّا غفر الله له فوق رأس كل مسلم سبعين ذنب ابن

An 'Abd Allah ibn 'Umar an rasul Allah salla Allah 'alayh wa sallam qal: ma min muslim yaghfir lil muslim illa ghafar Allah lahu fawq ra's kulli muslim sab'een dhanba

Narrated by Abdullah ibn Umar, The Messenger of Allah (peace be upon him) said: No Muslim forgives another Muslim, except Allah forgives him, above every Muslim seventy sins.

Source: Sunan Ibn Majah, Hadith No. 3680

Chapter 12:
Success and Ambition: Duas for Career and Personal Goals

Dua for Success in Work and Studies

ٱللّٰهُمَّ لَا سَهْلَ إِلَّا مَا جَعَلْتَهُ سَهْلًا وَأَنْتَ تَجْعَلُ الْحَزْنَ إِذَا شِئْتَ سَهْلًا

Allahumma la sahla illa ma ja'altahu sahla, wa 'anta taj'alul hazna idha shi'ta sahla.

Oh Allah, there is no ease except in that which You have made easy, and You make the difficulty, if You wish, easy.

Source: Sunan Ibn Majah 3435.

Story of Wisdom:

قَالَ إِنَّمَا أُوتِيتُهُ عَلَىٰ عِلْمٍ عِندِي ۚ أَوَلَمْ يَعْلَمْ أَنَّ اللَّهَ قَدْ أَهْلَكَ مِن قَبْلِهِ مِنَ الْقُرُونِ مَنْ هُوَ أَشَدُّ مِنْهُ قُوَّةً وَأَكْثَرُ جَمْعًا ۚ وَلَا يُسْأَلُ عَن ذُنُوبِهِمُ الْمُجْرِمُونَ

Qala innama ootitu hu 'ala 'ilmin 'indi. Awalam ya'lam anna Allah qad ahlaka man qablihi min alqurooni man howa ashaddu minhu quwwatan waaktharu jam'an. W la yusalu 'an dhunobihimu almujrimoon.

He said, "I was only given it because of knowledge I have." Did he not know that Allah had destroyed before him of generations those who were greater than him in power and greater in accumulation [of wealth]? But the criminals, about their sins, will not be asked.

Source: Surah Al-Qasas 28:78.

Dua for Barakah in Business

اللَّهمّ بارك لي في ما رزقتني

Allahumma barik li fi ma razaqtani

Oh Allah, bless me in what You have provided me.

Source: Tirmidhi 3370.

Story of Wisdom:

وَكاَن فِي الْمَدِينَةِ تِسْعَةُ رَهْطٍ يُفْسِدُونَ فِي الْأَرْضِ وَلَا يُصْلِحُونَ

Wa kaana fil-madinati tis'atu rahtin yufsidoona fil-ardi wa laa yuslihoon

And there were in the city nine family groups, causing corruption in the land and not amending [their ways].

Source: Quran 27:48.

Dua for Wisdom in Leadership

اللَّهُمَّ أَرِنِي الْحَقَّ حَقًّا وَارْزُقْنِي اتِّبَاعَهُ، وَأَرِنِي
الْبَاطِلَ بَاطِلاً وَارْزُقْنِي اجْتِنَابَهُ

Allahumma arini al-haqqa haqqan warzuqni ittiba'ahu, wa arini al-batila batilan warzuqni ijtinabahu

O Allah, show me truth as truth and bless me with following it, and show me falsehood as falsehood and bless me with abstaining from it.

Source: Jami` at-Tirmidhi 2447

Story of Wisdom:

قال رسول الله صلّى الله عليه وسلّم: من أراد أن دارا أن يستعين
على الأمور الدنيا والدّين والآخرة فليكثر السجود

Qaal Rasool Allahi salla Allahu 'alayhi wa sallam: Man arada an yasta'een 'ala al-umoor al-dunya wa al-deen wa al-akhirah falyukthir al-sujood

The Messenger of Allah, peace and blessings be upon him, said: Whoever wants support for worldly matters, religion, and the Hereafter, let him increase prostrations.

Source: Sunan Ibn Majah 3868

Dua for Overcoming Work Challenges

اللّٰهُمَّ ال سهل إلا ما جعلته سهلا وأنت تجعل الحزن إذا شئت سهلا

Allahumma la sahla illa ma ja'altu sahla, wa 'anta taj-alul hazna idha shi'ta sahla.

Oh Allah, there is no ease except in that which You have made easy, and You make the difficulty, if You wish, easy.

Source: Ibn Hibban in his Sahih #2426

Story of Wisdom:

قال رسول الله صلّى الله عليه وسلّم : إذا عملتم عملا فأتقنوه

Qala rasool Allahi salla Allah 'alayhi wa sallam : "Idha 'amiltum 'amalan fa'atqinuhu."

The Messenger of Allah, peace be upon him, said: "When you perform a deed, perform it with excellence."

Source: Sahih al-Bukhari, Kitab al-Iman, 56.

Dua for Prosperity and Sustenance

اللّٰهُمَّ اكفني بحلالك عن حرامك و أغنني بفضلك عمّن سواك

Allahumma kafini bihalalika 'an haramika wa aghnini bifadlika 'ammansiwaak

Oh Allah, suffice me with Your lawful against Your prohibited, and make me independent of all those besides You.

Source: Jami` at-Tirmidhi 3563

Story of Wisdom:

إنَّ : قال رسول الله صلّى الله عليه وسلّم
الله كتب الإحسان على كُلّ شيء

Qala rasool Allahi salla Allah alayhi wa sallam: Inna Allaha kataba al-ihsana 'ala kulli shay'

The Messenger of Allah said, "Verily, Allah has prescribed excellence in all things."

Source: Sahih Muslim 1955

Dua for Innovation and Creativity

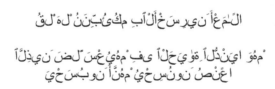

Allahumma aftah li abwaba rahmatika

Oh Allah, open the gates of Your mercy for me.

Source: Sunan Abu Dawood 5095.

Story of Wisdom:

قُلْ هَلْ نُنَبِّئُكُم بِٱلْأَخْسَرِينَ أَعْمَـٰلًا

ٱلَّذِينَ ضَلَّ سَعْيُهُمْ فِى ٱلْحَيَوٰةِ ٱلدُّنْيَا وَهُمْ
يَحْسَبُونَ أَنَّهُمْ يُحْسِنُونَ صُنْعًا

Qul hal nunabbi-ukum bil-akhsareena a'mala

Allatheena dalla sa'yoohum fil-hayatid-dunya wahum yahsaboona annahum yuhsinoona sun'a

Say, "Shall we inform you of the greatest losers in respect of their deeds? Those whose effort has been wasted in this life while they thought that they were acquiring good by their deeds."

Source: Quran 18:103-104.

Dua for Academic Achievement

اَللّٰهُمَّ لَا سَهْلَ إِلَّا مَا جَعَلْتَهُ سَهْلًا وَأَنْتَ تَجْعَلُ الْحَزْنَ إِذَا شِئْتَ سَهْلًا

Allahumma la sahla illa ma ja'altahu sahla, wa 'anta taj'alul hazna idha shi'ta sahla

Oh Allah, there is no ease except in that which You have made easy, and You make the difficulty, if You wish, easy.

Source: Sahih Ibn Hibban

Story of Wisdom:

قَالَ النَّبِيّ مُحَمَّد صَلَّى اللّٰه عَلَيْهِ وسَلَّم: إذا مررتم بكم
الجنّة فقولوا: اللّٰهُمَّ إِنِّي أَسْأَلُكَ الْعِلْمَ النافِع

Qala an-Nabi Muhammad sallallahu alayhi wa sallam: Itha marret bikum al jannah faqulu: Allahumma inni as'aluka al 'ilma an-nafi'a

The Prophet Muhammad (peace be upon him) said: When you come across the blessings, say: Oh Allah, I ask You for beneficial knowledge.

Source: Sahih Al-Bukhari 6471

Dua for Career Advancement

رَبِّ إِنِّي لِمَا أَنْزَلْتَ إِلَيَّ مِنْ خَيْرٍ فَقِيرٌ

Rabbi inni lima anzalta ilayya min khayr faqir

My Lord, indeed I am in need of whatever good you would send down to me.

Source: Quran 28:24

Story of Wisdom:

مَّثَلُ الَّذِينَ يُنفِقُونَ أَمْوَالَهُمْ فِي سَبِيلِ اللَّهِ كَمَثَلِ
حَبَّةٍ أَنبَتَتْ سَبْعَ سَنَابِلَ فِي كُلِّ سُنبُلَةٍ مِّائَةُ حَبَّةٍ ۗ
وَاللَّهُ يُضَاعِفُ لِمَن يَشَاءُ ۚ وَاللَّهُ وَاسِعٌ عَلِيمٌ

Mathalu allatheena yunfiqoona amwalahum fee sabeeli Allahi kamathali habbatin anbatat sab'a sanaabilin fee kulli sunbulatin miatu habbatin. Wallahu yuda'ifu liman yasha'. Wallahu wasi'un aleem

The likeness of those who spend their wealth in the Way of Allah, is as the likeness of a grain (of corn); it grows seven ears, and each ear has a hundred grains. Allah gives manifold increase to whom He pleases. And Allah is All-Sufficient for His creatures' needs, All-Knower.

Source: Quran 2:261

Dua for Protection from Unlawful Earnings

اللَّهُمَّ اكْفِنِي بِحَلَالِكَ عَنْ حَرَامِكَ وَأَغْنِنِي بِفَضْلِكَ عَمَّنْ سِوَاكَ

Allahumma kfini bihalalika 'an haramika wa aghnini bifadlika 'amman siwaka

Oh Allah, make Your lawful bounties sufficient for me so as to save me from what is unlawful, and from Your grace, make me independent of all others besides You.

Source: Sunan Ibn Majah, 3834

Story of Wisdom:

قال رسول الله صلى الله عليه وسلم: ما من يوم يصبح
العباد فيه إلا ملكان ينزلان فيقول أحدهما: اللَّهُمَّ أعط
منفقا خلفا، ويقول الآخر: اللَّهُمَّ أعط ممسك التلف

Qala rasool Allahi salla Allah 'alayhi wa sallam: Ma min yawm yusbihu al-'abadu fihi illa malakani yanzilani fa yaqoolu ahaduhuma: Allahumma 'ati munfiqan khalafan, wa yaqoolu al-akhir: Allahumma 'ati mumsikan talafan.

The Prophet Muhammad (peace be upon him) said: Every morning two angels descend and one of them says, "Oh Allah, compensate those who spend in Your cause" and the other says, "Oh Allah, bring destruction to those who withhold unduly."

Source: Sahih al-Bukhari, 1442

Dua for Job Satisfaction

اللَّهُمَّ لا سَهْلَ إِلَّا ما جَعَلْتَهُ سَهْلاً، وأنْتَ تَجْعَـلُ الحَـزْنَ اذا شِئْتَ سَهْلا

Allahumma la sahla illa ma ja'altahu sahlan, wa anta taj'alul hazna idha shi'ta sahlan

Oh Allah, nothing is easy except what You have made easy. If You wish, You can make the difficult easy.

Source: Sunan Ibn Majah 3835

Story of Wisdom:

قالَ رَسُولُ اللهِ صلّى الله عليه وسلّم "اذا نَفَرَ النَّاسُ مِنْ اِبْنِ آدَمَ فَيَزْدَادُ في عِنْدِ اللهِ حُبَّاً لَهُ، واذا تَبَاغَضَ النَّاسُ اِلى اِبْنِ آدَمَ فَيَزْدَادُ في عِنْدِ اللهِ بُغْضاً لَهُ"

Qala rasool Allahi salla Allah alaihi wa sallam "Itha nafara al-nasu min ibni adam, fayazdadu fi 'indi Allah hubban lahu, wa itha tabaghada al-nas ila ibni adam, fayazdadu fi 'indi Allah bugdan lahu"

The Messenger of Allah (peace and blessings of Allah be upon him) said, "When people are disliked by the son of Adam, he becomes more beloved in the sight of Allah. And when the son of Adam is hated by people, he becomes more disliked in the sight of Allah."

Source: Musnad Ahmad 23122

Dua for Balancing Work and Deen

اللَّهُمَّ إجعَلني خشيتِك كأنّي أراكَ، فإنّك تعلم أنّي لا أراكَ، وأعلم أنّك ترانِي

Allahumma ij'alni akhshyaka ka'anni araka, fa'innaka ta'lamu anni la araka, wa a'lamu annaka tarani

Oh Allah, make me fear You as if I see You, for indeed You know that I do not see You, but I know that You see me.

Source: Musnad Ahmad 16278

Story of Wisdom:

أَوَلَمْ يَسِيرُوا فِي الْأَرْضِ فَيَنظُرُوا كَيْفَ كَانَ عَاقِبَةُ
الَّذِينَ مِن قَبْلِهِمْ ۚ كَانُوا أَكْثَرَ مِنْهُمْ وَأَشَدَّ قُوَّةً وَآثَارًا
فِي الْأَرْضِ فَمَا أَغْنَىٰ عَنْهُم مَّا كَانُوا يَكْسِبُونَ

Awalam yaseerou fee al-ardi fayanthurou kayfa kana aqibatul-ladheena min qablihim? kanu akthara minhum wa'ashadda quwwatan wa'atharan fil-ardi fama aghna anhum ma kanu yaksiboon

Have they not traveled through the land and observed how was the end of those before them? They were greater than them in power and left a great impact on the land, but what they used to earn did not avail them.

Source: Quran 40:82

Dua for Guidance in Career Choices

اللّهُمَّ ارْزُقْنِي رِزْقًا حَلَالًا طَيِّبًا، وَأَعْطِنِي عَمَلًا مُبَارَكًا تَرْضَى بِهِ عَنِّي

Allahumma arzuqni rizqan halalan tayyiban, wa atini amalan mubarakan tarda bihi 'anni

Oh Allah, grant me a good and lawful provision, and bestow upon me a blessed job that You find satisfactory.

Source: Al-Mu'jam Al-Kabir 5706

Story of Wisdom:

قال رسول الله صلّى الله عليه وسلّم : اذا هم أحدكم بأمر فليركع
ركعتين من غير الفرض ثمّ ليقل اللّهُمَّ إنّي أسْتَخِيرُكَ بِعِلْمِكَ

Qala rasulullahi salla Allahu 'alayhi wa sallam: idha ham ahadukum bi-amr fal-yarka' rak'atain min ghayr al-fard thumma li-yaqul Allahumma inni astakhiruka bi-'ilmik

The Messenger of Allah (peace and blessings of Allah be upon him) said: "When any one of you is concerned about a matter, let him pray two Rak'ahs of non-obligatory prayer, then say: 'Oh Allah, I seek Your guidance in Your knowledge.'"

Source: Sahih Al-Bukhari 1166

Dua for Support in Entrepreneurial Ventures

اللَّهُمَّ انفعني بما علمتني وعلّمني ما ينفعني وزدني علما

Allahumma anfa'ni bima allamtani wa allimni ma yanfa'ni wa zidni 'ilma

Oh Allah, benefit me with what You have taught me, teach me what will benefit me, and increase me in knowledge.

Source: Jami` at-Tirmidhi 3599

Story of Wisdom:

عَنْ عَائِشَةَ، قَالَتْ قَالَ رَسُولُ اللَّهِ صلى الله عليه
وسلم ,, مَا ضَرَّ بَعْدَ الْيَقِينِ شَكٌّ,,

An 'Aa'ishah, qalat qala rasoolu Allahi salla Allah 'alayhi wa sallam "ma darra ba'd al-yaqini shakkun"

Narrated by Aisha, she said the Prophet Muhammad (peace be upon him) said, "No doubt after certainty is harmful."

Source: Sahih al-Bukhari 52

Chapter 13:
Bonus Chapter: Words of Inspiration for Exceptional Circumstances

Dua for Comfort in Times of Loss

اللّٰهُمَّ إِنِّي أَعوذ بك من هَمَزة الشّياطين وأعوذ بك رَبِّ أن يحضرون

Allahumma inni a'udhu bika min hamazat ash-Shayateen, wa a'udhu bika Rabbi an yahdhuroon

O Allah, I seek refuge with You from the whisperings of the devils, and I seek refuge with You, O Lord, lest they be present with me.

Source: Sahih al-Bukhari 3281

Story of Wisdom:

قال رسول الله صلّى الله عليه وسلم: إذا مات الانسان انقطع عمله إلّا من ثلاثة: صدقة جارية، أو علم ينتفع به، أو ولد صالح يدعو له.

Qala rasool Allahi salla Allah alayhi wa sallam: "Idha maat al-insan inqata'a amaluh illa min thalatha: sadaqatin jariyah, 'aw 'ilmin yuntafa' bih, 'aw walad salih yad'u lahu."

The Prophet Muhammad (peace be upon him) said: "When a person dies, his deeds are cut off except for three: ongoing charity, beneficial knowledge, or a righteous child who prays for him."

Source: Sahih Muslim 1631

Dua for Hope in Difficult Situations

اللّٰهُمَّ رَحْمَتَكَ أَرْجو فَلا تَكِلْني إلى نَفْسي طَرْفَةَ عَيْنٍ وَأَصْلِحْ لي شَأْني كُلَّهُ لا إِلهَ إِلّا أَنْتَ

Allahumma rahmataka arju, fala takilni ila nafsi tarfata 'aynin, wa aslih li sha'ni kullah, la ilaha illa anta.

128

Oh Allah, I hope for Your Mercy. Do not leave me to rely on myself even for the blink of an eye. Correct all of my affairs for me. There is no God but You.

Source: Abu Dawud

Story of Wisdom:

عَنْ أَبِي هُرَيْرَةَ قَالَ قَالَ رَسُولُ اللَّهِ صلى الله عليه
وسلم الْكَيِّسُ مَنْ دَانَ نَفْسَهُ وَعَمِلَ لِمَا بَعْدَ الْمَوْتِ وَالْعَاجِزُ
مَنْ أَتْبَعَ نَفْسَهُ هَوَاهَا وَتَمَنَّى عَلَى اللَّهِ الأَمَانِيَّ

'An Abi Hurayrata qala qala Rasulullahi salla Allahu 'alayhi wa sallam al-kayyisu man danan nafsahu wa 'amila lima ba'da al-mawti wal-'ajizu man atba'a nafsahu hawaha wa tamanna 'ala Allahi al-amaniyya.

Narrated by Abu Huraira, The Prophet, peace be upon him, said: "The wise man is the one who calls himself to account and performs deeds for what comes after death; the incapable is the one who follows his desires and then entertains hopes in Allah's mercy."

Source: Sunan Ibn Majah

Dua for Strength During Illness

اللَّهُمَّ رَبَّ النَّاسِ، أَذْهِبِ الْبَأْسَ، اشْفِ أَنْتَ الشَّافِي،
لَا شِفَاءَ إِلَّا شِفَاؤُكَ، شِفَاءً لَا يُغَادِرُ سَقَمًا

Allahumma Rabban-nas adhhibal-ba'sa, ishfi anta Ash-Shafi, la shifa'a illa shifa'uk, shifa'an la yughadiru saqaman

O Allah, Lord of mankind, remove the affliction, Heal for You are The Healer, there is no healing but Your Healing, a healing that will leave behind no ailment.

Source: Sahih al-Bukhari 5743

Story of Wisdom:

عن أبي هريرة قال: قال النَّبِيّ صلى الله عليه وسلَّم: ,,
لا يُؤْمِنُ أَحَدُكُمْ حَتَّى يُحِبَّ لِأَخِيهِ ما يُحِبُّ لِنَفْسِهِ ,,

An abi Hurayrah qal: qal al-nabi salallahu alayhi wasalam: "La yumenu ahadukum hatta yuhibba li akhihi ma yuhibbu li nafsih"

On the authority of Abu Hurayrah who said: the Prophet (peace be upon him) said: "None of you truly believes until he loves for his brother what he loves for himself."

Source: Sahih al-Bukhari 13

Dua for Perseverance in Trials

اللهم لا سهل إلا ما جعلته سهلا وأنت تجعل الحزن إذا شئت سهلا

Allahumma la sahla illa ma ja'altahu sahlan, wa 'anta taj'alul hazna idha shi'ta sahlan

O Allah, there is no ease other than what You make easy. If You please You ease sorrow.

Source: Sunan Ibn Majah 3435

Story of Wisdom:

قال النبيّي صلّى الله عليه وسلّم: ,,عجبا لأمر المؤمن إنّ أمره كلّه خير وليس ذاك لأحد إلا للمؤمن إن أصابته سرّاء شكر فكان خيرا له وإن أصابته ضرّاء صبر فكان خيرا له''

Qaal an-Nabiyyu salla Allahu 'alayhi wa sallam: "'Ajaban li-amr al-Mu'min, inna amrahu kullahu khair. Wa laysa dhaaka li-ahadin illa lill-Mu'min. In asabathu sarraa shakara fa kaana khairan lahu. Wa in asabathu darraa sabara fa kaana khairan lahu."

The Prophet Muhammad (peace be upon him) said, "How wonderful is the case of a believer; there is good for him in everything and this is not the case with anyone except a believer. If prosperity attends him, he expresses gratitude to Allah and that is good for him; and if adversity befalls him, he endures it patiently and that is better for him."

Source: Sahih Muslim 2999

Dua for Renewal of Faith

اللهم يا مقلب القلوب ثبت قلبي على دينك

Allahumma Ya Muqallibal Qulubi, Thabbit Qalbi 'Ala Deenik

Oh Allah, Controller of hearts, make my heart firm upon Your religion.

Source: Sunan At-Tirmidhi 2140

Story of Wisdom:

قال النبيّ صلّى الله عليه وسلّم : من سلك طريقا
يلتمس فيه علما سهل الله له به طريقا إلى الجنّة

Qala an-Nabiyy sallallahu alayhi wa sallam: Man salaka tariqan yaltemisu fihi 'ilman, sahalallahu lahu bihi tariqan ila al-Jannah

The Prophet (peace be upon him) said: Whoever treads a path in pursuit of knowledge, Allah will make easy for him a path to paradise.

Source: Sahih Muslim 2699.

Dua for Discovering Life's Purpose

اللّهُمَّ أرِني الحقَّ حقًّا وارزقني اتّباعه، وأرِني
الباطل باطلًا وارزقني اجتنابه

Allahumma arini al-haqqa haqqan warzuqni ittiba'ah, warini al-batila batilan warzuqni ijtinaabah

Oh Allah, show me the truth as truth and grant me the following of it, and show me falsehood as falsehood and grant me the avoidance of it.

Source: Jami` at-Tirmidhi 2567

Story of Wisdom:

قال النبيّ صلّى الله عليه وسلّم: إنّما بُعِثْتُ لأتمِّم مكارم الأخلاقْ"

Qaal an-Nabi salla Allah alayhi wa sallam: "Innama bu'ithtu li-utammima makarimal-akhlaq"

The Prophet (peace be upon him) said: "I have been sent to perfect good character."

Source: Al-Muwatta Malik 47.1.8

Dua for Accepting One's Destiny

اللَّهُمَّ إِنِّي أَسْأَلُكَ الْهُدَىٰ وَالتُّقَىٰ وَالْعَفَافَ وَالْغِنَىٰ

Allahumma inni as'alukal-huda wat-tuqa wal-'afafa wal-ghina

O Allah, I ask you for guidance, piety, chastity and self-sufficiency.

Source: Sahih Muslim 2721

Story of Wisdom:

عَنْ أَبِي هريره رضي اللہ عنہ أن رسول اللہ صلّى
اللہ علیہ وسلّم، قال: إذا أحبّ اللہ عبدا ابتلاه

'An Abi Hurairah radi allahu 'anhu 'an rasul allahi salla allahu 'alayhi wa sallam, qal: 'Idha 'ahaba allahu 'abdan ibtalah

Narrated Abu Hurairah may Allah be pleased with him that the Messenger of Allah peace be upon him said: When Allah loves a servant, He tests him.

Source: Sahih al-Tirmidhi 2396

Dua for Joy and Happiness in Life

اللَّهُمَّ أدخل على أهل القبور السرور

Allahumma adkhil 'ala ahlil-quboori-suroor

Oh Allah, bring joy to the people of the graves.

Source: Jami` at-Tirmidhi 3540

Story of Wisdom:

عَنْ ابن عبّاس رضي اللہ عنهما أن رسول اللہ صلّى
اللہ علیہ وسلّم، قال : من سرّہ أن يبسط لہ في
رزقہ، وینسأ لہ في أثرہ، فلیصل رحمہ

'An ibn 'Abbas radiyallahu 'anhuma anna rasoola Allahi salla Allah 'alayhi wa sallam, qaal : man sarrahu an yabsut lahu fee rizqihi, wa yunsa' lahu fee atharihi, falyasil rahimahu

Narrated Ibn 'Abbas: The Messenger of Allah (peace be upon him) said: He who desires that his provision be expanded and his term of life be prolonged should maintain good ties with his kin.

Source: Sahih al-Bukhari 5985

Dua for Maintaining Hope for Improvement

اَللّٰهُمَّ لَا سَهْلَ إِلَّا مَا جَعَلْتَهُ سَهْلًا، وَأَنْتَ تَجْعَلُ الْحَزَنَ إِذَا شِئْتَ سَهْلًا

Allahumma la sahla illa ma ja'altahu sahlan, wa anta taj'alul hazna idha shi'ta sahlan.

O Allah, there is nothing easy except what You make easy, and You make the difficult easy if it be Your will.

Source: Tirmidhi 3502

Story of Wisdom:

قَوْلُهُ تَعَالَى: فَإِنَّ مَعَ الْعُسْرِ يُسْرَا، إِنَّ مَعَ الْعُسْرِ يُسْرَا

Qawluhu ta'ala: Fa'inna ma'al 'usri yusra, Inna ma'al 'usri yusra.

Allah Most High says: So, verily, with every difficulty, there is relief. Verily, with every difficulty there is relief.

Source: Quran 94:5-6

Dua for Spiritual Renewal

اللّٰهُمَّ اي مُقَلِّبَ الْقُلُوبِ وَالْأَبْصَارِ ثَبِّتْ قَلْبِي عَلَى دِينِكَ

Allahumma Ya Muqallibal Quloob Wal Absaar, Thabbit Qalbi 'Ala Deenik

Oh Allah, The Turner of hearts and sights, make my heart firm upon Your religion.

Source: Sahih Muslim 2654

Story of Wisdom:

قَالَ مُوسَىٰ لِقَوْمِهِ اسْتَعِينُوا بِاللَّهِ وَاصْبِرُوا ۖ إِنَّ الْأَرْضَ
لِلَّهِ يُورِثُهَا مَن يَشَاءُ مِنْ عِبَادِهِ ۖ وَالْعَاقِبَةُ لِلْمُتَّقِينَ

Qala Moosa liqawmihi ista'eenu billahi wasbiru. Inna al-arda lillahi yoorithuha man yashao min ibadihi. Wal-aqibatu lilmuttaqeen

Moses said to his people: "Seek help through Allah and be patient. Indeed, the Earth belongs to Allah, He gives it to whom He wills of His servants. And the end result is for the righteous."

Source: Quran 7:128

Dua for Liberation from Guilt

اللَّهُمَّ أَنْتَ رَبِّي لَا إِلَٰهَ إِلَّا أَنْتَ خَلَقْتَنِي وَأَنَا عَبْدُكَ وَأَنَا عَلَىٰ عَهْدِكَ
وَوَعْدِكَ مَا اسْتَطَعْتُ أَعُوذُ بِكَ مِنْ شَرِّ مَا صَنَعْتُ أَبُوءُ لَكَ بِنِعْمَتِكَ
عَلَيَّ وَأَبُوءُ لَكَ بِذَنْبِي فَاغْفِرْ لِي فَإِنَّهُ لَا يَغْفِرُ الذُّنُوبَ إِلَّا أَنْتَ

Allahumma anta Rabbi la ilaha illa anta, khalaqtani wa ana 'abduka, wa ana 'ala 'ahdika wa wa'dika ma astata'tu, a'udhu bika min sharri ma sana'tu, abu'u laka bini'matika 'alayya, wa abu'u laka bidhanbi faghfir li, fa innahu la yaghfiru adhdhunuba illa anta.

O Allah, You are my Lord, there is none worthy of worship but You. You created me and I am Your servant, and I abide by Your covenant and promise as best I can, I take refuge in You from the evil of my deeds. I acknowledge Your favor upon me and I acknowledge my sin, so forgive me, for verily none can forgive sins but You.

Source: Sahih al-Bukhari 6306

Story of Wisdom:

عَنْ أَبِي هُرَيْرَةَ، قَالَ قَالَ رَسُولُ اللَّهِ صَلَّى اللَّهُ عَلَيْهِ وَسَلَّمَ ‏"‏ إِذَا
أَرَادَ اللَّهُ بِعَبْدِهِ الْخَيْرَ عَجَّلَ لَهُ الْعُقُوبَةَ فِي الدُّنْيَا وَإِذَا أَرَادَ اللَّهُ
بِعَبْدِهِ الشَّرَّ أَمْسَكَ عَنْهُ بِذَنْبِهِ حَتَّى يُوَفِّيَهُ يَوْمَ الْقِيَامَةِ

An Abi Hurayrah, qala qala rasool Allah salla Allah alayhe wa sallam "Idha arad Allah bi 'abdihi al-khair 'ajjala lahu al-'uqubah fi al-dunya wa idha arad

Allah bi ʿabdihi al-shar ʿamsaka ʿanhu bi dhanbihi hatta yuwaffiya bihi yawm al-qiyamah."

Abu Huraira reported: The Messenger of Allah, peace and blessings be upon him, said, "If Allah intends good for someone, then he hastens the punishment for them in this world, and if Allah intends evil for someone, then he withholds their sins from them until he recompenses them for it on the Day of Resurrection."

Source: Jami` at-Tirmidhi 2396

Dua for Protection During Social Unrest

شر رعلا بّر تنأو ،تلكّوت كيلع ،تنأ ألإ هلإ ال هللا تنأ مَهللا
ألإ ةوّق الو لوح الو ،نكي مل أشي مل امو ،ناك هللا ءاش ام ،ميركلا
دق هللا نأو ريدق ءيش لّك ىلع هللا نأ ملعأ ،ميظعلا يلعلا بالله
رّش نمو ،يسفن رّش نم كب ذوعأ ينّإ مَهللا ،املع ءيش لّكب طاحأ
.ميقتسْمُ طارص ىلع يبّر نّإ ،اهتيصانب ذخآ تنأ ةبّاد لّك

Allahumma Anta Allah, la ilaha illa Ant, ʿalayka tawakkalt, wa Anta Rabbu'l-arshil karim, ma shaʾ Allah kan, wa ma lam yashaʾ lam yakun, wa la hawla wa la quwwata illa billahil ʿaliyyil ʿazim, aʿlamu anna Allah ʿala kulli shayʾin qadir wa anna Allah qad ahaat bikulli shayʾin ʿilma, Allahumma inni aʿudhu bika min sharri nafsi, wa min sharri kulli dabbah Anta akidhun bi naasiyatiha, inna rabbiy ʿala siratim mustaqim.

Oh Allah, You are Allah, there is no deity but You, upon You I rely, and You are the Lord of the Noble Throne. Whatever Allah wills is, and what He does not will, is not. There is no power or strength except with Allah, the High, the Great. I know that Allah is capable of everything and that Allah surrounds all things in knowledge. O Allah, I seek refuge in You from the evil of myself, and from the evil of every creature You are grasping by its forelock. Surely my Lord is on a straight path.

Source: Sunan Abi Dawood 1523

Story of Wisdom:

عن أبي هريرة رضي الله عنه عن النبي صلى الله
عليه وسلّم قال: (يقول الله تعالى: إذا أحبّ عبدي
لقائي أحببت لقاءه، وإذا كره لقائي كرهت لقاءه)

'An abi hurayra radiyallahu 'anhu 'an al-nabiyi sallallahu 'alayhi wa sallam qal: (yaqolu allah ta'ala: idha 'ahabba 'abdi liqa'i, 'ahabbtu liqa'ahu, wa idha karih liqa'i, krahtu liqa'ahu)

Narrated on the authority of Abu Huraira (may Allah be pleased with him), the Prophet (peace be upon him) said, "Allah the Almighty says: If My servant loves to meet Me, I love to meet him; and if he dislikes to meet Me, I dislike to meet him."

Source: Sahih al-Bukhari 6507.

Disclaimer

The information presented in this book, "The Journey of Prophet Muhammad: Discovering Islam Through the Quran | Duas and Insights for a Meaningful Muslim Life," is intended for general informational purposes only. The content is based on historical and religious sources, and every effort has been made to ensure its accuracy.

Readers are advised to consult with qualified religious scholars, experts, or other authoritative sources to verify the interpretations and understandings presented in this book. The author and the publisher do not assume any responsibility or liability for the accuracy, completeness, or usefulness of the information provided herein.

This book is not intended to serve as a substitute for professional religious guidance or scholarly opinions. Individual beliefs and practices may vary, and readers are encouraged to seek personal guidance from qualified religious authorities to address their specific circumstances.

The author and the publisher disclaim any responsibility for any loss, injury, or damage resulting directly or indirectly from the use or application of the information contained in this book. Readers are urged to exercise their own judgment and discretion when applying the teachings and insights discussed in this book to their own lives.

The views expressed in this book are those of the author and do not necessarily reflect the official stance or opinions of any religious institution or organization. The book is a personal exploration and interpretation of the teachings of Prophet Muhammad and the Quran.

By reading this book, readers acknowledge and accept the limitations of the information provided, and they are encouraged to engage in further research and consultation to deepen their understanding of Islam and its teachings.

BONUS

Dear Reader,

We thank you for supporting us in carrying the message of Allah to the world.

We regularly have further updates on other projects and would be happy if you subscribe to our newsletter:

A positive surprise and our thanks are waiting for you.